CU00731631

LILAC AND R(
Our home in the Cév

EDITOR'S NOTE

P eg, my mum, first went to France in 1938 as her 'year out' before teacher training college. She stayed with the Marcus family – Georges and Géllo – and was *au pair* to their daughter Monique. They had an enormous influence on her, and it was because of them that her love affair began with the country, its people, their attitude to life and especially food!

She wrote this book in 1975 and my dad, Al, helped type it. It was sent to several publishing houses. They all seemed of the same opinion that no-one would be interested in the story of an English family buying and doing up an old house in France. A decade or so later, the whole world had heard of Peter Mayle!

After my parents' deaths, I desperately wanted to keep the 'old pile' going, gave up work and went into the *gîte* business. I slightly edited – and published – a small number of copies of the book with love and gratitude for all they gave me.

Now, in March 2001, I am delighted that the Léonie Press has decided to publish it 'properly' – 25 years after those original publishers turned it down.

Jan Bevan
March 2001

LILAC AND ROSES
OUR HOME IN THE CÉVENNES SUN

La Clède, Ardèche 1963-1974

PEGGY ANDERSON

an imprint of
ANNE LOADER
PUBLICATIONS

Dedicated to "la Grande Hélène"

ISBN
1 901253 22 8

Published March 2001

© Jan Bevan

Typeset and published in Gt Britain by:
Léonie Press
an imprint of
Anne Loader Publications
13 Vale Road, Hartford,
Northwich, Cheshire CW8 1PL
Tel: 01606 75660
Fax: 01606 77609
e-mail: anne@leoniepress.com
Webesite: www.leoniepress.com

Printed by:
Anne Loader Publications

CONTENTS

Peggy and Alan Anderson in 1965

FOREWORD

Our friends thought we were mad when we bought a ruined farmhouse. We were not unique in wanting a country home, but our ruin was 800 miles away in France!

This is the story of that house, of its painfully slow conversion to a summer home, of the changes we saw in the beautiful Ardèche village where it is situated and, lastly, of the affluent years between 1964 and 1974 as we saw them.

P A

CHAPTER 1

HOW TO BUY A HOUSE
WITHOUT REALLY TRYING

We went down to the only tennis court after lunch to find four people already knocking up. On a hot, rather sultry afternoon, almost at the end of our holiday, it meant we were at a loose end for the first time.

It was August 1963. Alan, my husband, and I were staying at a hotel in Aubenas in a region of France practically unknown to the English, even to many French. North of Nîmes, west of Montélimar, on the edge of the Cévennes, it is a region of mountains, forests and small tributaries which all eventually flow into the beautiful Ardèche river.

I'd had the good fortune to have a year in France as part of my education and could speak the language well. Since 1950 we'd always spent some part of our holidays in France with the kids. Though we knew many areas well, until 1963 we'd never heard of the Ardèche and had arrived in Aubenas by accident from Provence, which we were exploring on a tip given us the previous year while away on our own for once.

In 1962, my son Ian was in Spain and we'd dropped our daughter Jan with the family of her pen pal, Françoise, in Montpellier. The family was so charming and welcoming that we left Jan confident she'd enjoy her two weeks with them. Meanwhile, we were planning to spend a week in the Pyrénées, but first a week in a country hotel near Carcassonne which had been especially recommended to us.

We've never since been back to this remote hotel. Perhaps we were afraid to lose a magic memory. The address said Cuxac-Cabardès, a romantic enough name, which turned out to be a small village about 2kms off the Carcassonne-Mazamet main road. We were directed by the postman to a narrow road

1

which climbed through the forest. From time to time we'd pass a tree with a red arrow and the word Hotel. After about a mile the hard road stopped.

"Where now?" said Alan.

"Over there?" I said, pointing to another arrow towards a forest track. "But surely it can't be right. We're in the middle of nowhere."

As we bounced along the rough track, I wondered what I'd let us in for. Alan leaves all the holiday arrangements to me and I usually pick out something good. This looked most unpromising. The path eventually opened out on to a terrace in front of a large house. We got out of the car and went dubiously through the open door.

We were met by an overwhelming smell of fruit. On every surface – tables, chests and window ledges – were trays of melons, peaches, pears and apricots. The walls were wood-panelled and mounted with hunting trophies, notably wild boar heads.

"Do you think this is it?" I was just whispering to Alan when the proprietor came in.

"Mr and Mrs Anderson, good evening," she said, holding out her hand.

"Good evening, Madame. What a wonderful hall this is!"

"Yes, as you may have guessed, this used to be a hunting lodge. My parents bought it, but I could not afford to live here without taking guests. Come, I will show you your room."

We followed her up the beautiful staircase which curved round three sides, forming a gallery above.

We soon realised why this hotel had been so strongly recommended. For a week we feasted on superb country cooking. Lunch was always served on the terrace. All around us stretched the forest. Within a twenty-mile radius among chestnuts and pines we found peaceful, hidden valleys. We fell in love with this new countryside, swimming alone and naked in rocky rivers, exploring villages often totally deserted. We began to wonder if it would be possible to buy one of these remote houses. They were all solidly built of stone, some in quite reasonable condition.

"It's no good," said Alan, "having to go miles to get things we need."

Grudgingly, I admitted we'd be better off in a community, that we were too conditioned to a certain level of comfort to let ourselves in for an isolated, primitive life.

"We must have water and electricity," I said. "The other things are less important, but without those, life would be difficult."

The following week we fell in love with a different countryside as we explored Prades and Font-Romeu, the valley of the Tech and the Canigou, a very noble mountain. We were surprised to find that at this height it was only just warm enough to have breakfast on our balcony. During the day it was wonderful, too hot to be active between midday and three, but in these narrow valleys the sun disappeared quite early in the evening, leaving a temperature more suited to brisk walking than strolling.

One morning, drinking an *apéritif* in a café, we started chatting to a local man, who, once he'd established that we weren't German, was disposed to be friendly.

"We love it here," I said. "I don't suppose you know if there are any village houses for sale in the area?"

"That's my office over there," he said, pointing across the road. "I'm an estate agent." We should never have guessed. There was no sign, nothing to indicate his profession – about him or his 'office'.

"Actually I do know of one house which is being renovated. It's nearly finished. Would you like to see it this afternoon?"

We were delighted to say yes, but very disappointed when we saw the house. It was in a square opposite a massive church and couldn't have been more than eleven feet wide. It had been smartened up, judging by its neighbours, and was a triumph of ingenuity and planning inside. It was like a lighthouse, kitchen on the ground floor, living room on the second, reached by a spiral staircase which continued upward to a bedroom and a minute bathroom. There was no garden or space for a car, not even a balcony.

"It can't possibly cost much," I whispered to Alan. But it turned out they wanted 32,500F (about £2,500).

"They must have thought we were American," I said to Alan over dinner that night.

"Yes, from Texas," he replied. "This is obviously an expensive area. We'll have to look elsewhere."

"There must be something, somewhere between a deserted village and a fashionable place like this," I said.

When we went to collect Jan, it was Monsieur Alméras, Françoise's father, who drew an arc around south eastern France, assuring us that anywhere within that area we should have a true Mediterranean climate. On his advice we decided to visit Provence the following year, as Jan and Françoise had agreed to repeat their exchange.

And that's how we ended up there. We stayed in a delightful village, well back from the expensive coast, called Moustiers-Ste-Marie. There was another noble mountain, the Ventoux. The gorges of the Verdon were spectacular, but the countryside was disappointing. Apart from the lavender fields, the land was sun-baked and arid and the small rivers dried up. For three days under a burning sun we shivered in the fiendish *mistral* wind; then it began to rain. On the second rainy day, rather disillusioned with Provence, we set off, a little aimlessly, up the old N7.

Before the *autoroute* was built, this main highway from Paris to the south fully deserved its bad reputation. Before long we were sitting helplessly in the pouring rain in a traffic jam, just outside Montélimar. After ten minutes of breathing petrol fumes and sickly nougat I got out the map and said to Alan, "I don't care where we go but we must get off this dreadful road."

At the first opportunity we turned left across the Rhône and found ourselves in the Ardèche.

We had a very late lunch at Privas, then climbed over a high pass with stunning views down to Aubenas. As we drove down the valley the sun came out to greet us and showed us green countryside, a pleasant change from the yellowed slopes of Provence.

"There's a good hotel just out of Aubenas called La Pinède. I wonder if we'll be able to get in," I said, closing the Guide Michelin. "Let's try it."

This hotel has since been mentioned several times in the British press as a good centre for exploring the Ardèche, "that beautiful but little known region of France." In 1963 full board was 22F a day with the exchange rate at 13F to the pound! The food was wonderful and far too copious. We always sent back as much as we ate. Madame Mazet also served the largest *apéritifs* in France. Before lunch and dinner we were always installed on the terrace drinking enormous Cinzanos.

The countryside was beautiful, very similar to that around our hunting lodge the previous year – chestnut and pine forests with rocky rivers and stone villages. We usually played tennis in the morning, but two days before we were due to go home, it was drizzling slightly so we didn't go down until the afternoon. We found the court in use, and Alan said, "What would you like to do instead? Shall we try to find an estate agent to survey the field a bit here before we leave?"

We'd already discovered in Provence that estate agents were hard to find. In rural France, property tends to stay in the family. Even when a sale is desired, it's quite often arranged by word of mouth. We'd not seen one in Aubenas so set off to nearby Vals les Bains. After several enquiries we found an agent in a large block of flats, where he used a room in his apartment as an office.

There was another client ahead of us. As we waited in the hall we couldn't help overhearing two female voices and every word that was spoken. One voice was offering for sale a cottage needing renovation in a village about 8kms south of Aubenas. The other was apologising for her husband's absence and saying that she would make a note of the property and ask him to visit later. When the two women came out I could hardly wait to explain our situation.

"May we come and see your house, Madame?"

"Well, I came to town by bus. I can't show you until tomorrow."

"Could we possibly give you a lift home and see it this afternoon? We'll be going home to England the day after tomorrow."

Our offer was accepted. We thanked the agent's wife, who said she had only one other house on her books and that it was quite a distance away. In the car, the woman explained that she was staying with her cousin in this village called Fons. She and her husband had always intended to renovate the old house for their retirement.

"Unfortunately," she said, "my husband died last year and I don't think I could face country life alone. I have decided to stay in Paris. No-one has lived in the cottage for years. My cousin uses it as a store."

Fons was a hamlet rather than a village, 3kms off the main Aubenas-Alès road. It was quite pretty, a cluster of stone houses, a small square, a church, vineyards and a stream. We couldn't see a café or any shops as we wandered around waiting for her to get the keys. There was no-one about. Complete silence reigned as we followed her down a little road of houses, propped up one against the other. She turned into a small yard and up a flight of stone steps, opened a heavy old door and we stepped inside.

It was hot, stuffy and dark until we got the shutters open. The window was small but let in enough light to show us a hearth, a stone sink and many bales of hay. Near me was a second door to another room. I opened it. Two black and white rabbits were through the gap before I could close it. In that brief moment I could see at least a dozen more rabbits, hopping around more bales of hay. The woman, obviously country born and bred, disappeared and came back with some lettuce leaves. With these she soon caught the escapees and we all quickly slid through the gap into the other room where the rabbits, seemingly quite tame, carried on munching and ignored us. It was not exactly easy to look round, but we mentally registered three habitable rooms, two facing south, roof apparently sound, floors doubtful. We asked about water and electricity.

"There is a cold tap down below. I'll show you." We went out and down the steps into the yard. A heavy door opened on to a vaulted, stone-flagged store where we saw the tap as well as piles of boxes, sacks, buckets and dozens of empty wine bottles. There was another door ahead of me but I was more cautious this time. All the same, I imagine you could have heard my yelp of surprise all over the village when I found myself face to face – this time with an enormous bull!

The south-facing garden ran along the side of the road down to the stream. Beyond were fruit trees and vineyards. The garden was full of vegetables, well watered and cared for.

"The electricity is just here in the road," she said. "The baker calls four times a week, the butcher once, and you have the supermarket on the main road."

We were then invited to her cousin's house for a 'glass'. This turned out to be mint syrup, with icy water added which was most welcome and refreshing. The cousin's house had been renovated and was austerely furnished. When we began to talk money, things got complicated. When discussing property, people to this day still talk in old francs, i.e. in hundreds. We had to get it worked out in writing before we got the correct figure, 6,000 new francs, or £500 approximately. We finished our drinks, thanked both women and bowed ourselves out, promising to call back the next day with a decision.

We were very excited and talked about our find all through dinner. I kept saying, "Are you sure we can do something with it?" knowing that I often got carried away on a wave of enthusiasm.

"I don't think we can go wrong," said Alan. "The site and

stone alone are worth the money, even if we almost have to rebuild the house."

"Is the price right though? Shall we make an offer?"

"Well, I think it might be a good idea to go back to Vals tomorrow and ask the agent if he'll come with us to look at it again."

Next morning I asked Alan if he'd had second thoughts.

"No, I think it's worth going for."

"Come on then, we haven't much time left."

The agent was very surprised to see us so early, especially as we were interested in a house he hadn't even known existed until late the previous evening, but he agreed to come with us.

"We're sorry to rush you," I apologised, "but we're only here on holiday and have to go home tomorrow."

"I don't deal much in old property," he said as we got into the car. "Most of my work is in Vals and Aubenas. I own quite a lot of property here actually, including this block of flats." And he waved his hand back at the imposing block we'd just left. We felt almost guilty for involving him in this obviously small-fry deal and I hastily said, "It's extremely kind of you to give us your time. We know nothing of the market here and will be most grateful for your opinion."

After inspecting the little house with us, his opinion was that we could buy it with confidence. "By spending something in the region of 12,000F on it, you should have a nice little holiday home." At the same time, however, he urged us, before finally deciding, to see the other old house which his wife had mentioned. "You really should see it to compare the two."

"How much is it?"

It was exactly double and in a village 25kms away. We really didn't want to go. It was hot and uncomfortable in the car and we'd much rather have gone for a swim on our last day. Alan looked at me. "I suppose we'd better go, just in case. He's being very helpful."

It was a dull, hot road. Not until we turned off it, at a little town called Joyeuse, did we see forests again. We were driving by the side of a river. After 5kms or so we turned left up a much narrower road. We climbed steeply through chestnut groves and vineyards, occasionally passing a grey stone house and catching sight of a pretty church set high above us as the road twisted and turned – there were two severe hairpin bends. We parked finally in a small square in front of the church as there was no more hard road.

"Don't worry," said the agent, as we walked along the dirt track between beautiful stone walls enclosing vines, "they're going to continue the hard road right through the village soon."

We walked past a group of houses and rounding these stood in a narrow lane looking up at what appeared to be two houses joined by a stone arch. There was an old wooden board fixed to the wall which read *Danger de mort*. In my head I immediately translated it as "This is a death trap!"

"It's all right," laughed the agent, noticing my worried face "that's just to keep people away." We went under the arch, up some steps and on to a terrace with a roof sagging heavily over it. There were two doors, one facing us and one on our right, and all the windows were tightly shuttered. Neither of the doors would open with the two enormous keys the agent produced. Then a neighbour appeared wanting to help (and find out what was going on!), produced some oil and finally got us inside. As at the other house, it was dark and stuffy until we got the windows and shutters open. The sun streamed in through iron bars and broken panes. The floor was cement, the plaster crumbling off the walls. The beams were covered in flaking grey paint and cobwebs. It was like a prison cell, but it had been occupied and quite recently, it appeared. There was a large bed, made up, with a crucifix on the wall above and a candlestick on the table beside it. In the corner of the room was a huge fireplace, with the remains of a fire in the hearth, a trivet and a saucepan. There was a round table, four small cane chairs and a bench. Two rooms led off from this one, both empty, grey and depressing, with the same barred windows.

There were no stairs but both rooms had solitary electric bulbs hanging from one of the beams.

We went back into the first room, passed through a heavy old door, and down some stone steps into the other wing of the house. This was Cinderella land – the original kitchen with another massive fireplace, a stone sink with a built-in cupboard above and a cool cupboard. The floor was stone-flagged, the beams black with soot. Off this room was another one with a vaulted ceiling, an old iron bedstead perched precariously on a rotten wooden floor, and in one corner an old brass tap barely attached to the wall.

Back in the old kitchen was an extremely decrepit wooden ladder-type staircase. "Do you want to go up?" said our guide. "Be careful, it's probably rotten."

Gingerly, we climbed up. The room above was pitch black, the small windows blocked, the stone walls encrusted with black soot. As our eyes adjusted we could see that parts of the roof were missing. The floor looked none too safe there either, and at the far end of the room it suddenly ended, as did the top of the chimney of the fireplace below.

"This is odd," said Alan. "There must have been a fire in here sometime."

"This is the *clède*, said the agent. This was a new word to me but I was too busy to pursue it as I peered into the adjoining room, which seemed to have a solid floor, and then renegotiated the stairs. We were all standing again in the old kitchen. As I looked round, I began to get the feel of the age of the house (about 200 years old the agent had told us). Cleaned up, this would be a lovely room. I came down to earth when I realised what our friend was saying.

"Of course, this side doesn't really count. You must concentrate on the other. There you already have three quite good rooms. Come, I'll show you the granary where you can make bedrooms."

We went outside again on to the terrace, down the steps, across a small courtyard, and up again on to a kind of cat-walk at the side of a derelict building with very little roof left.

"Was this part lived in too?" I asked.

"Oh no, that was the *soirerie*."

This I did understand and explained to Alan I'd read about the cottage silk industry (which had grown up around Lyon in the 19th century). As we climbed through the terraces at the side of the house, Alan pointed out a mulberry tree. "More evidence," he said.

To get into the granary, we had to walk over some old pine trunks which crossed a deep ditch, full of broken tiles and old stones, all overgrown with bramble and weed. The granary was quite empty. It had thick beams of untrimmed pine, but there was ample headroom and the roof tiles seemed sound here and the floor solid. There were two shuttered and barred openings at the back and three at the front – no windows. We had a lovely view of the village from up here over the caved-in roof of the silkhouse. To our left was the church, sited prominently to overlook the valley; grey mountain ranges filled the horizon in the far distance. Small groups of stone houses built haphazardly amongst the vineyards dotted the hillside sloping down in front of us with paths and tracks twisting through them. The opposite slope of the valley was covered with pines. In the beautifully clear air we could actually see the electricity wires stretched between poles on the crest, taking civilisation to other remote mountain villages.

The vineyards looked immaculate, the houses well maintained. There was an air of wellbeing about the village. Outside again at the back of the house, the agent waved vaguely to the left to the neglected terraces of land at the side of the house.

"There's quite a lot of land. Four *faïisses* here (a word I took to mean levels – a local dialect word, I discovered later) and three more above the road as far as that cherry tree." There seemed to be about half an acre in all. Alan and I turned from scanning the 'garden' to see the agent mopping his brow.

"What we all need," I said, "is a drink. Can we get one in the village?"

"Yes, just down there ," he said pointing towards an elegant turreted house. "At the *château*. But we must take the car. It's too hot to walk."

Just before leaving the property, Alan said we had to look inside the doors (to the cellars he assumed) off the courtyard which he'd seen as we crossed to go to the upstairs granary. These were rotten and offered no resistance. We all went inside to discover a wonderful cool. We studied the thick walls, the vaulted ceilings.

"This isn't going to fall down in a hurry," Alan said. "It'll certainly see me out!"

We sat outside under some beautiful shade-giving plane trees and drank *pastis*. There were huge tubs of hydrangeas all along the walls. The girl who served us looked at us with curiosity but with a large smile. The agent began to talk fast. I had to concentrate hard because he had a very strong and unaccustomed accent and I had to keep translating for Alan. This apparently was the café/shop/post office. There was a baker and several travelling shops. In Joyeuse, 7kms away, there was everything we would need – large shops, solicitor, doctors, chemists, hotels, school and hospital. I began to ask about work which would have to be done on the house.

"There are several builders and a carpenter here in the village. You should start by knocking down the small ruin, install proper light, water and sanitary arrangements. It will be easy to make a staircase and there is ample room for three bedrooms upstairs. By spending about 20,000F you will have a lovely home."

I should have liked to go back for another look at the house but it was getting near that sacred lunch hour and we had 25kms to drive. We dropped the agent back in Vals and promised to call the next day on our way home.

We were late for lunch but nobody seemed to mind. It was an excellent one as usual, I suppose, but for once we barely noticed. We had far too much to talk about. I think we both immediately discarded the idea of buying the first cottage. The second house was obviously a much better bargain, but it would take all our money. I should have to be responsible for paying the renovation costs (as it was my dream), which meant committing myself to a full-time job for many more years. With two children wanting university education, we had expensive years ahead.

"Supposing I'm ill and have to stop working," I said, already thinking the worst. "I'm sure we could always sell it half-finished if we had to," said Alan. I felt Alan was really as enthusiastic as I.

"I'm going to offer them 10,000F, take it or leave it," he said, trying to appear casual. "If they want more, too bad. Do you agree?"

And that's what we did. In the morning, we turned the car north, calling in at Vals which was on our way. The agent seemed to think that our offer would be accepted and phoned a solicitor in Joyeuse who said he would act for us if necessary. We thanked him very much for all his help, shook hands and left.

We were both rather quiet as we drove up the beautiful Ardèche valley towards Le Puy. My thoughts were not altogether happy. In all we had seen the house for about twenty minutes. We'd had no time to explore the village or Joyeuse. Had we been too impetuous? Today, £900 doesn't seem a lot of money but in 1963 it was not something to be lightly squandered. Perhaps we were crazy.

This thought was confirmed a little later by my sister Sheila, who went to see what we should get for our little nestegg. She was on her way home to Geneva from Spain with her family. A short detour would take them through 'our' village. I'd written suggesting they should go and see it.

At home the days and weeks went by with no word from the agent or my sister. At last came an envelope with the familiar Swiss stamp. Sheila wrote that they had driven up to the village and enquired at the café about the house for sale. They were directed to 'our' house and were utterly appalled by this dreadful ruin with its sagging roofs, rotten shutters and barred windows. As they were standing aghast in the courtyard, a neighbour appeared. He told them that there was no point looking around as the house was sold.

"I think you've had a lucky escape," she wrote. Our immediate reaction was a mixture of relief and disappointment and we tried to forget the whole business. I wondered where we could start looking next year. Three days later the contract arrived by post with a letter from the solicitor asking us to arrange payment as soon as possible. The house was indeed sold – but to us!

I suppose we could have pulled out. We hadn't signed anything or parted with any money. I'm not usually one to chance my arm, but Alan seemed very sure that all would be well and we both had a hunch that we must seize this opportunity which had come our way so unexpectedly.

"How to buy a house without really trying!" I said as I signed the contract. My dream had come true. I had my house in the sun.

CHAPTER 2

FIRST MOVES

L ike my sister, most of our friends too thought we were mad. Sometimes during the winter of 1963/64, I wondered if they were right. I tried several times to draw a plan of the house but could never get it quite right. I could remember the greyness, the flaking plaster, the iron bars and that dreadful sagging roof over the terrace but not the size of the rooms or the position of the windows.

"Stop worrying," Alan would say, "It's built like a cathedral. Remember the vaulted ceilings in the cellars and the stonework on the front." I had to agree we'd bought something solid. I went over our list of essentials: climate, water, electricity, access to shops – everything was right.

It would have helped if our friends had said "How exciting!" when we told them about our venture. Mostly they asked how we hoped to get any work done, or supervise it, from 800 miles away. As we were having quite a lot of trouble getting anyone to do a bit of paving and make us a terrace for our old Edwardian house in England, we were rather concerned about this ourselves. During the winter I started a special account with £150. I saved hard in order to have money in hand before the bills started coming in. Meanwhile, nothing was thrown away. If we replaced anything in the house, the old article was put away "for France." I used Green Shield stamps for cutlery, kitchen equipment and linen. I looked out bargains at jumble sales. All this helped me to hang on to the feeling that we'd done the right thing, even though I couldn't remember clearly what my house was like!

We could remember it well enough to know that there was no question of living there for the whole of our summer holiday, but we decided to risk camping there for one week between a week's stay at two different local hotels. Jan would be with us the first week before going on to her French family at Montpellier. Naturally, we went first to our great find in Aubenas, La Pinède.

Very early on the first day we were at the agent's asking for the keys. He said we'd find them with the solicitor in Joyeuse and also recommended us a surveyor. We decided to visit him the following day and set off for Joyeuse, the solicitor and the keys.

We remembered Joyeuse vaguely as a small country town, important only because the main Alès road passed through its high street. We barely recognised it when we arrived. It was full of cars and there didn't seem to be anywhere to park. Eventually someone drove off and we were able to slip into the space. The high street was thronged with people. We were directed to the solicitor down a very steep hill which led to a large square lined with plane trees. Immediately we understood the reason for the crowds. It was market day. Everyone from every village within 20kms must have been there as well as holiday makers and dozens of children from summer camps with their student minders. It was tempting to have a good look round this animated scene but we passed behind the stalls into a quiet road off the square. The solicitor's office was easy to find and we stepped into a cool, tiled hall. After explaining to a secretary who we were and what we wanted, we were shown into a room which was straight out of a Dickens novel. It was all there – ancient furniture, a hat stand, a grandfather clock. A quill pen would not have been out of place on the huge desk, whose top was piled with papers, ledgers and files. Everything in the room was faded and dusty. Behind the desk stood the solicitor, charming, courteous and welcoming, but absolutely blank about keys. He looked equally baffled when I mentioned our birth and marriage certificates which had been necessary for the sale.

"We'll gladly collect those later," I said, "but we are rather anxious to have the keys now to go and see the house we've bought!"

He pulled out a drawer, lifted it out completely and tipped the contents on top of the piled-up desk. There must have been six or seven dozen keys in every conceivable shape and size, some tied together with string but not one marked or labelled in any way.

"Choose, Madame," he said! We looked at each other and tried to cast our minds back. We needed one about 8 inches long, heavy, preferably rusty. We picked out four and left as quickly as good manners allowed, promising to return later to finalise things.

The drive up to the house was prettier than we'd remembered, the village well cared for as we'd noticed the year before. The house looked even more neglected and derelict than on our first visit. We tried all the keys in both the doors leading off the terrace. We heaved and pushed, wondering if the terrace roof would fall down and kill us with all the banging and shaking that was going on. We got very hot and very cross and made no impression at all!

After about five minutes of this we all three (Jan was with us) sat on the wall to cool off. I looked at the barred and shuttered windows, realising that it was hopeless to try to get in that way.

"I'm damned if I'll be beaten!, said Alan, suddenly getting up. He stood facing the door, took a run and gave the door a mighty kick, just like a tough cop in a film. The door burst open. We were in.

It was stifling inside. We quickly went right round and opened all the shutters in each of the three rooms of the newer wing. Nothing had changed. The bed, the table and chairs, the crucifix, the candlestick, the ashes in the hearth – all there exactly as we'd seen them a year ago. I suppose the furniture had not been considered worth taking away, but to us it was invaluable. The bedstead was solid mahogany. The chairs had seen better days but two of them were hand- made. We didn't recognise the wood of the table but it was solid and had obviously been made by a local carpenter. We'd brought two single beds and camping gear, so together with what we'd inherited, we could be comparatively civilised.

We started to unload the car. Everything had to be carried from the road, now tarmaced, through the narrow opening under the stone arch, up the terrace steps and into the kitchen. It was hot work. We put the last box on the kitchen floor, pulled the door to and only then realised that we couldn't relock it.

"I've forgotten the word for locksmith," I said.

"Don't worry," said Alan. "If I can buy the right things, I can fix it."

We had to leave it at that for the time being. Most unexpectedly, we'd been invited to *apéritifs* to meet the solicitor's wife and family. There were three daughters, two teenagers and a girl of 21, one of the most beautiful women I've ever seen. She was in her second year at Lyon University reading law. She spoke English quite well and Alan was delighted to be able to chat to her! Jan practised her French with the other two whilst I explained our breaking and entering exploits to Monsieur and Madame.

"But what made you come to the Ardèche in the first place? Even the rest of France barely knows we exist!" said Madame.

"It was a complete accident," I said. "Actually we bought the house because we couldn't play tennis one day." I realised immediately how frivolous that sounded and gave them a quick account of that most unusual day last year. How we had discovered the Ardèche, the house and how much we loved it already.

We were advised to go to Vedel, the big hardware shop off the high street, for our new lock and left thanking them all for their kindness. The market was over. Joyeuse was a sleepy provincial town again. We went into the first restaurant we saw and had a cheap meal. At 2.30pm we were at the door of the hardware store waiting for them to open. It was an unusually large establishment for such a small town with a most helpful owner. In the end my French failed me completely (I'd had no previous occasion to want to fit a new lock) and we were reduced to drawing pictures before Alan had all he needed.

He had a very difficult time with that wretched door. It had dropped several inches and it was near impossible to get things even.

"I don't think I'm going to be able to manage this," he said, sweat dripping off his ears. But he returned to the job with his usual persistence and at last got both sides level.

We were gradually to learn that each such "little job" had its special problems in this house. Nothing was ever simple or easy. On that day we had no idea of what was in store and felt quite elated as we finally turned the key in the lock and set off back to Aubenas and the hotel. For the first time I think we felt that this pile of old stones really belonged to us.

The next day we set off again to find Monsieur Crozier, our *mettreur* (surveyor). He could speak no English, but he had a very pleasant, quietly professional manner and a much less heavy accent than the house agent. We explained who had sent us and that we wanted advice about an old house we'd bought. I was still a little apprehensive about our ruin and anxious to be reassured in spite of Alan's confidence. When the surveyor turned to me after a thorough inspection and said, "Madame, you have not been robbed," I could have hugged him! I was even happier when I saw him standing in the little road looking up at the end wall of the old kitchen wing with obvious admiration.

"This dressed stone is really beautiful."

So, when the blow fell, it was the more unexpected. Although he agreed in principle with the agent about concentrating on the newer wing, he said, "It is vital that you reroof this old wing first. It really is dangerous. And you must get rid of all this," he said, pointing to the roof over the terrace. "You can leave the terrace open here. Reroof the newer side only if you wish; it's sound as it is. If you pull down this lean-to at the same time as the stone arch and the derelict building there, you'll be able to extend your terrace right to the end to over-look the road. It will be spacious – at least ten metres long."

"If that's your opinion, I suppose we must do it," I said, but couldn't hide my disappointment from Alan. It seemed very hard that we must first spend a lot of money on demolition and reroofing just to gain extra terrace space. I was wanting to get on with the part of the house where we should live. (In retrospect, of course, he was quite right. The whole point is that one spends most of one's time outside). Just then, the builder, Georges Balazuc, turned up. We'd discovered that he lived just along the road and that our neighbour opposite, Monsieur Toral, worked with him.

This really was an unexpected stroke of luck. Once the three men got together, Alan and I became superfluous. Monsieur Crozier explained his ideas. The builder looked very dubious. He seemed to think the whole wing might come down if they disturbed the lean-to. In the end they decided that they would try.

Way ahead of myself, as usual, I was already imagining myself sitting on my new terrace enjoying the view which would be revealed when the old silkhouse was gone. Monsieur Crozier said he would draw up some plans; the other two promised to do the roof before the following Easter.

"We'll come at Easter, won't we?" I said urgently to Alan. I was determined to be there to push them on to the next stage. Meanwhile, we said goodbye, informing them we intended to camp in the house the following week. As we dropped Monsieur Crozier off in Aubenas we were again surprised to be invited in for a drink. Madame Crozier asked practically all the same questions as the solicitor's wife. How had we found our way to the Ardèche? Why did we want a house there?

"The Belgians and Dutch come here but very seldom any English. And where did you learn to speak French so well, Madame?"

I explained. "And, of course, in no time at all, your husband will pick it up and be speaking just as fluently." She beamed at us both. Alan made a face. He had finished with French at Inter level a long time ago and, fairly naturally, was content to leave the talking to me. I was quite confident that, in the end, he would speak well because he had such a wonderful ear – much keener than mine.

After a few more words about the plans, we left and drove up to the hotel.

"Wasn't that nice?" I said. "You know, the French don't usually invite strangers into their homes. It was very kind of them. I guess they must be really curious, but I feel so welcomed? Do you?" Alan agreed. It seemed like a good beginning.

For the rest of the week we forgot about the house. We played tennis. We showed Jan some of the good swimming places we'd found the previous year. We went up into the mountains to escape the heat. On these trips, we seldom saw anyone, just occasionally another car, or an old woman minding her goats. Not once did we pass a car with a GB plate. This green, delightful countryside seemed to belong to us.

Early on Saturday morning, we drove Jan down to Montpellier and the Alméras family and came straight back to move into our new home. We turned on the water, installed the gas cylinder, and our new 3-burner cooker was soon boiling water. Meanwhile, we attacked every surface with brooms and scrapers. The dirt and cobwebs of countless years filled many buckets. Then we washed down every ceiling, wall and floor with hot water, soap and disinfectant. The whole place smelled clean. The old red quarry tiles in the middle room responded nobly to our efforts, but washing cement floors is a tiring and unrewarding task. By 8pm we were exhausted. We'd been wearing shorts and shirts and suddenly realised, as we switched on our few naked bulbs, that we were both covered in grey dust and plaster from head to foot.

We stripped off and sluiced down in turn in a bowl of hot water. There was an inch of grey sludge in the bowls when we emptied them. We put on clean clothes and felt renewed except our throats were dry and mouths parched since we'd breathed a lot of dust too. This we remedied by eating a huge picnic on the still warm terrace – *pâté*, salad, cheese, fruit, a whole *baguette* and the best part of two bottles of wine!

We covered the now dry tiles in the middle room with a huge plastic sheet, put down our two mattresses and, just as we were, fell sound asleep within seconds. Waking up was very odd. It really was rather like a dungeon, with the barred windows, the patchy plaster and the mattresses on the floor, but of course we weren't locked in and were soon drinking coffee and eating bread and marmalade in the hot sun outside.

That morning we made a detailed inspection of all that we'd inherited in the way of furniture and equipment. As well as the pieces already mentioned, we'd found two tables in the old kitchen, one horribly wormeaten, but the second one in fair condition with a useful drawer. There were also pans, bowls, some china, cutlery and a coffee pot. It was rather like Robinson Crusoe salvaging things from the wreck. We threw nothing away which could possibly be put to some use. The mattress on the old bed had to go with other miscellaneous junk, and the courtyard was soon full of the oddest assortment of furniture and household goods airing in the sun. We sat with another coffee and decided how best to arrange everything.

We brought the two bases for our single beds into the middle room. The wormy table was covered with some old cretonne fabric to serve as our dressing table, with a jug and basin, Victorian-style. We even had two old rugs for the floor. We fixed a clothes line along one wall and put our clothes on hangers. The bedside table went between the beds with a kitchen chair at each side and we were almost 3-star!

We had a dreadful struggle to get the old mahogany bedstead into the far room, which we intended to use as our bedroom the following year. It weighed a ton and we only just managed to get it through the doorways without scraping all the skin off our knuckles. The first room with the fireplace was obviously to be our kitchen/living room for the time being. The table with the drawer was just big enough to hold a washing up bowl, a draining board and our 3-burner cooker with the gas bottle and a bucket underneath. We put our few kitchen tools and cutlery in the drawer.

Blessing the window ledges in the 3ft-thick walls, I arranged my pans on the one at the front near the cooker, my bits of china on the one at the back, with the surplus on the mantelpiece. We had our good round table and chairs plus bench and folding canvas chairs (for comfort) and a matching canvas lounger, which we used both inside and out. We'd had one very bright thought and had brought a wall food safe, which held our small stock of food and was vital as we felt pretty sure we must have mice, if not rats!

We'd also brought an assortment of brooms, a bread bin, bowls, jugs and so on, but one of the major items was an elegant pale blue and white, heavy plastic Elsan (chemical toilet). It had been packed with china and linen as it travelled in the boot of the car, much to the customs official's surprise, and was now set up in the old kitchen of the other wing. (Of all the things about a primitive life, this was the one thing I really hated, actually preferring the garden. I was absolutely overjoyed when we were able to discard it when we eventually got our septic tank and proper loo).

There was no light in the old kitchen, so a trip after dark necessitated taking a candle. This unlived-in, 200-year old, soot-covered room was unbelievably eerie by candlelight. Rather than go there, I preferred to perform my final pee in the courtyard. There was an outside bulb on the terrace which shed quite a lot of light. One night I squatted down while Alan went up the steps to turn on the light. To my surprise when the light came on I found myself face to face with a giant toad. We were both in approximately the same position; he seemed quite disinclined to move; I couldn't for a bit. He just watched me without batting an eyelid.

Alan found it very amusing. He always teased me about the loo. "Even the Queen has to use one on aeroplanes, dear."

"I don't suppose anyone else is allowed to though," I added.

At that time I doubt if there were many flush toilets in the village, but I determined to have my usual mod con at the earliest possible opportunity.

It would be an exaggeration to say that we were comfortable that summer of '64. All water had to be carried from the one cold tap through the old kitchen. All waste water had to be thrown away outside. It was impossible to keep the place dust-free. Preparing a meal was difficult with no work surface except the table and a minimum of kitchen tools, but it was much better than a tent or caravan and fun for a few days. We counted ourselves lucky.

Gradually we realised just how lucky! We got to know our neighbours the Torals across the road better. They were of Spanish origin – almost illiterate. They could read but barely write and spoke with a heavy accent. They had somehow saved enough money to buy the old building opposite for the same price as ours and were gradually making it more comfortable. They had a very large family. One son and daughter were still at home and various grandchildren stayed during the school holidays. They also had several dogs, cats, chickens, geese and rabbits and very little money.

Their garden was at the other side of their house, large and well cared for. Whenever they picked anything for themselves, something was brought to us. Only at my absolute insistence was I allowed to pay a few francs for potatoes, onions, beans, tomatoes, pears or peaches warm from the sun. We had only to ask. If they had it, they lent it – spade, screws, clothes pegs, saw – anything. We were very touched by such genuine kindness and goodwill to complete strangers.

We also soon realised our great good fortune in arriving in this particular village. Often in the evening we went for a short walk. We explored the road behind the house which disappeared up into the forest. The higher one went, the more extensive were the views over the whole valley. The complete stillness and the clean smell of the pines were very welcome after a hard, hot day.

In the other direction the road passed more houses before curving round the mountain. I shall never forget the view the first time we went round the bend in the late evening. A long way below we could see the river curving in and out. The land fell down to it in terraces of chestnut groves, olive trees and vines, with huge rocks projecting occasionally, and everywhere the pattern of stone retaining walls. On the floor of the valley were orchards and vineyards. On the other side of the river, another road, more vineyards, then a high cliff of rock with a few houses clinging to it. Above these, range after range of mountains stretched away to right and left catching the last golden rays of the sun which was setting behind us. It was a splendour of greens and gold with no sound except the continual chirp of the *cigales*.

We stood there entranced. How could we have been so lucky? The following day we had to go and investigate the river. We took the car down to the road to Joyeuse but turned left at the bridge and continued up the valley. The signpost said Valgorge 14kms. We drove all the way, following the river. It was stunning and enchanted us both – lots of wonderful places to swim. Luckily two of the best were also the nearest.

Only a few hundred yards from the signpost was a beautiful natural pool. It was rather difficult to scramble down the rocks off the road, but once down, you could dive off into ten feet of water, swim up river for forty yards or cross over to a sandy beach on the opposite side. The water was so clear that you could see fish swimming way below you, and so warm that you could sit with it up to your neck and read! The greatest joy was that, apart from one fisherman, there was nobody there.

We had good swimming the following week at our next hotel in Les Vans. It too was listed in the Michelin but we were more than pleasantly surprised when we arrived. The approach was through peach groves and led to a small château! We should have retraced our steps had not the name been well posted all along the road. The inside of the hotel was very much out of the ordinary. The entrance hall was lofty and cool, with a curving stone staircase. The antique furniture in the salon looked very much at home. Our bedroom had a magnificent four-poster. The food was well prepared and presented but much less copious that at La Pinède. We made friends with a charming Dutch couple who spoke near perfect English and usually spent our mornings with them on the river beach.

This was the second delightful surprise of Le Scipionet. The Chassezac, another tributary of the Ardèche, ran through the grounds, which meant private swimming. There was a small sandy beach and enough water for a gentle swim around, though it didn't compare with the deep pool in our own river. We were told that the last of three dams had just been completed on this river and that the flow of water was controlled. We decided to do the circular trip to the top dam, up one side of the Chassezac and down the other. It was a most impressive drive. I suppose the valley was even more beautiful before the dams were built, but the roads were not there before, so part of it must have been inaccessible. The new lakes were very attractive, lapping against the steep rocky sides of the mountains, but most important of all, I suppose, was the electricity it produced.

I'm not altogether on the side of those who protest so violently about the ruination of the countryside. We'd just spent a week in rather primitive conditions, which had made us realise how hard life must have been in these remote rural areas in the old days. One of my clearest early memories of our village is of our baker, cooling off outside his house at 8am wearing nothing but a pair of shorts, his bare shoulders powdered with flour. We loved to watch him pushing the long wooden paddles into the oven to get out his *flutes*. Now he has a beautiful new shop, with an automatic lift to bring the bread up from the bakehouse beneath, a huge refrigerated display case for butter, cream and cheese, as well as a freezer for icecreams. He wouldn't want to go back to his wood-burning oven and enormously heavy bread baskets. Nor would the farmers' wives want to give up their washing machines and fridges. Washing at the public *lavoir* may look romantic in the summer when it's pleasant to linger and gossip with the neighbours, but it's less appealing in winter with the water icy cold. The blessing of electricity has made life so much easier. Even the remotest farms seem to have access to light and power – quite an engineering feat.

As we were leaving the hotel to go back to our primitive life, Ian my son turned up on his scooter. We'd been half expecting him as we knew he'd very much wanted to see the house. Back home in our village the next day we drove right up our valley and he immediately fell in love with the Ardèche as we had done. We went swimming daily and walked up into the forest. As we stood in the same spot, in the cool of the evening, where Alan and I had first realised that it was a very kind fate which had sent us to Ribes, Ian said, "It's not fair, is it? There are so many people who will never see anything as beautiful as this." As Jan too had given her full approval to everything, we were delighted.

When we were going to bed that night, Alan said, "You know, I like my children very much."

"So do I," I replied. "We're very lucky and I'm so pleased they like it here."

The next morning, just the same, I got very impatient with Ian. He didn't really want to leave, although he knew he ought to be on his way – he had a vacation job waiting in England. We had to urge him to get going in order to be ready for the Alméras family, who were shortly arriving with Jan and Françoise.

We were taking Françoise back to England with us this year. I was rather alarmed at having to make lunch for six people in such uninviting conditions but I did my best. We ate home-grown leeks (courtesy of Madame Toral), rolled in ham with *vinaigrette*, cold roast chicken, salad, cheese and chocolate mousse – all with three *flutes* and three bottles of local wine. And it was quite a success, which pleased me enormously. Madame Alméras had always received us royally in

Montpellier and it was thanks to her husband, indirectly, that we had arrived here.

Looking back, I think the Alméras realised better than we did just exactly what we'd taken on. They looked apprehensively upwards as they walked under the terrace roof. "Yes, your surveyor is right. You certainly must get rid of this – it's very dangerous," said Monsieur Alméras.

"You'll have to take it a little at a time," said his wife. "There's a lot to do."

Perhaps they too thought we were a little crazy. But we didn't care!

CHAPTER 3

GETTING TO KNOW
THE LOCAL PEOPLE

C razy or not, we began to plan during the winter. Loath as I was to abandon the original old kitchen with its enormous fireplace and stone-flagged floor, I'd reluctantly accepted that we should have to begin our renovation in the newer wing of the house. It was obvious that we could make a good kitchen, a bathroom/bedroom and a living room from the three existing rooms. Later on, the granary above would give three good bedrooms. I consoled myself thinking that one day I might be able to do the old wing too.

The main problem was that we couldn't commission a complete conversion. As the bills were all to be paid out of income, the work had to be done in stages. We had to decide on our priorities, bearing in mind a general idea of what we wanted to achieve in the end. First essentials were a working kitchen, a bathroom, a bedroom for ourselves and a sleeping space for visitors. As the house was to be no more than a holiday home until at least 1970, bare necessities would be provided first; frills and luxuries were in the distant future.

In considering basics for the kitchen, we made our first mistake. We wanted to cover the cement floor with ceramic tiles, but decided to postpone that and settled temporarily on grey vinyl. When we eventually reorganised the kitchen six years later, ceramic tiles were five times the price and we couldn't afford them! Temporary often became permanent we were to find!

We decided to ask Geo, the builder, to fit us a plain white sink and water heater in the kitchen and a shower and basin in the end room. If this could be done between Easter and summer, we could set about the other work ourselves. The nicest thing about our present kitchen in England was its size – sixteen foot by twelve. We had a peninsula breakfast bar, lots of cupboards and an adjacent laundry room. In France, we'd an even larger area, seventeen foot by fourteen, but of course it would have to serve as a dining room too for many years.

Even in a purely working kitchen I'm not too keen on a totally clinical look, but in a dining kitchen a sunny, friendly atmosphere is important too. At the same time it's possible to strain too much after atmosphere at the expense of convenience and practicability. Few people then would have wanted to keep a stone sink and wooden worktops and draining board needing to be scrubbed regularly. Even the most ardent traditionalist wouldn't want to cook everything on an open fire, as had the last owner, just to retain the authentic touch (an Aga was expensively out of the question), and there was no way of preventing a fridge, a cooker, or washing machine from looking modern. When all this is said, what usually decides things for most people is the cost, and so it was with us.

We couldn't afford to pay a carpenter to make us shelves and cupboards in pine which is what we really should have liked. We had to find something we could do ourselves. Alan was quite an old hand at decorating but knew nothing about carpentry. However, a friend had given him a beautiful set of tools, and with these and his trusty Black and Decker, he was prepared to have a try at anything. We discovered DIY flatpack kits for cupboards and decided on chipboard covered with heavy-duty Fablon to make cheap shelving and worktops. We needed as much light as possible with our rather small windows and decided on a yellow and white scheme. We'd sand down the beams, paint the walls pale yellow and the cupboards white. But this would have to wait until summer.

At Easter, we packed the car with everything we could think of to add to our comfort: more china, kitchen equipment, an old electric fire, fabrics and bedding, plus lots of Easter eggs for the children of friends and neighbours – and on the roof a single bed.

On the high plateau after Le Puy, old snow was lying in drifts but there were patches of blue sky. We could feel the temperature rising as we drove down the valley. At Aubenas it was warm and in Ribes a truly perfect day. As we approached the house, I could see the builder and our neighbour on the roof.

"Oh, look, they're there working," I said to Alan, beaming from ear to ear. Rushing from the car, I climbed the steps and called *"Bonjour!"* The old roof overhanging the terrace was gone and I was standing in full sunshine. The door and shutters were open. Inside everything was neat and tidy. When I saw a little vase of lily of the valley on the table, a lump came to my throat and I knew that our lovely, kind neighbour, Madame Toral, had been in. By the time we'd unloaded the car, it was midday; the men had shouted *"Bon appétit"* and departed. It was cold in the house and a joy to set up our folding chairs and table and eat our picnic lunch in the sunshine, even though we couldn't see much except our own neglected land and the derelict building opposite.

We hit our first problem when we switched on the electricity and got no light. Alan tried the bulbs and fuses. Everything seemed to be in order.

"I just don't understand it," he said, "we'll have to find an electrician."

"Let's make up the beds first and unpack," I replied, "then we'll go into Joyeuse and try to find someone to sort it out."

Five o'clock found us in the electrician's high street shop in Joyeuse. It was very well stocked with fridges, washing machines, light fittings – all mod cons, in fact. When we explained that we had no light at all, he said he would come immediately to have a look. We had several more jobs to do in town and then intended to stay on for dinner somewhere, so I said, "We can manage with candles tonight, but we'd be pleased to see you early tomorrow morning."

We ordered a new mattress for the old mahogany bed, did

some food shopping, then set off to find a newsagent. We found one in a little square where we hadn't been before; it was in the older part of the town above the high street. Not surprisingly, there were no English papers, but the proprietor promised to order them for the summer. We were intrigued to see on the opposite side of the square a painter and signwriter's shop with the unlikely name of O'Fairbuck over the door!

Taking up one whole side of the square was a hotel with a round stone tower at one end, the walls all covered in creeper, and tables set out in front of the main entrance. We ate there for 9F a head plus 1.50F for a bottle of local wine. The pleasant young couple in charge told us that the owner and his wife would be arriving from Paris the following day.

All was bustle and activity for us the following morning. Geo, his brother, Serge, and neighbour, Monsieur Toral, were tiling the roof. At 9 o'clock a plumber and mate arrived, set up a work bench in the yard and began manipulating some zinc which was to go in the angle of the roof. A few minutes later, Monsieur Saboul, the electrician, arrived. What a team going for us! I felt exhilarated!

The young plumber was unusually tall for a Frenchman, well-built and very handsome; the electrician short and thick-set. The working uniform seemed to be a navy string vest plus a pair of shorts or jeans and *espadrilles*. Everybody worked, sweated and chatted, but above all looked happy doing it – except the electrician. He just looked extremely puzzled. Eventually, he came back with his ladder from the back of the house and announced, "Someone has cut the main cable!" We had quite literally been cut off! Who on earth had done that? Nobody could offer an explanation.

"I'll go back to Joyeuse," said Saboul, "and ring up the electricity people in Largentière, tell them I'm going to repair it. I suggest you go there in person this afternoon ."

As we'd not been to this town before, we were quite pleased to go and do a little exploring. It was well worth the trip. We found a truly mediaeval town surrounded by walls and gates and incredibly narrow streets. It was set in a deep ravine with an enormous castle high on a hill and a river at the foot of the old walls. The electricity headquarters were pointed out to us on the far side of the river about 2kms away. It looked an imposing building but when we arrived it was locked up, completely deserted. We sat waiting, admiring the spectacular view in the absolute stillness of a warm afternoon. The sound of a vehicle chugging up the hill broke the silence. A van stopped outside the main door of the building and from it stepped a man in conventional working overalls, who fished behind a shutter and opened the door with a key that was obviously always kept there. As it seemed that afternoon work had now begun, we followed him inside.

I'd just begun my explanation when he said, "One moment, please, Madame," and disappeared! A few minutes later a door marked *Bureau* opened and there was our same man in a smart blue uniform, complete with peaked cap with gold band.

"Please come in and be seated, *Monsieurdame.*"

We sat down, trying not to laugh and to adjust to the required formality, but couldn't hide our astonishment when he told us that they, the authority, had cut the cable.

"You did!" I exclaimed, "but why?"

"Well, Madame, I regret there is an unpaid bill," he said.

"How can there be? We haven't used any!" I answered rather crossly.

"No, Madame, it is outstanding since the owner died seven years ago. The inheritors have not paid us."

"But it's nothing to do with us," said Alan in English to me. "Why should we pay it?"

"If we don't, I don't think we'll get any juice."

"How much is it?" I said to the man. When he said 12.50F (about £1 then), I couldn't believe my ears! I got the money out of my purse and put it on the desk in front of him.

"We'll pay it. Are there any other problems?"

"You are supposed to have a new meter which you must pay

for." We explained that we were here for only four more days, that we would gladly have the new meter installed in the summer, but could we please use the existing one temporarily?

"Certainly, Madame, that will be quite all right," he said.

"And you won't cut us off again, will you?" I said as we got up to go.

"Certainly not, Madame."

We sat in the car for a few minutes in disbelief, grumbling about nationalised industries in general and this one in particular. We were just going to set off when our man came out, in overalls again, put the key behind the shutter, gave us a wave and set off down the hill!

"We must have honest faces," said Alan. "We could raid the joint! Come on, let's go see what progress the electrician's made." So, we took our honest, hopeful faces back to Joyeuse and parked outside Saboul's shop.

"I've fixed it," he said delightedly. "Next month, I'll come up and put you some decent lighting in. "

"And some power points too, please," I said. "Meantime, what do we owe you?"

"Oh, don't worry about that now. You can pay me when I've finished in the summer."

"Fine," I smiled, "and thank you so much for helping us out."

We wandered off up the high street. It was fairly busy. I remembered that it was Easter Saturday and people were doing their shopping for the weekend. I hadn't much to buy beyond bread and milk, as we'd booked a table for dinner at our newly discovered hotel with the tower, La Récluse, and we'd been invited to Sunday lunch by Madame Balazuc, mother of Geo, our builder. We finished our bit of shopping and drove round to the little square which was full of cars. We just managed to squeeze in, sat ourselves down at a table outside the hotel and ordered drinks.

We were enjoying the evening sun, a feeling of achievement and watching the general, pre-dinner bustle, when who should arrive but our handsome young plumber. To our great surprise, he greeted us with a huge smile, shook us warmly by the hand and invited us to the bar for a drink. Before we could draw breath, we were inside being introduced to everybody, including the proprietor and his wife, and found ourselves the centre of interest as our friend explained that we were the English couple who had bought a house in Ribes.

We met Monsieur O'Fairbuck, and his wife – we recognised her as our solicitor's secretary – and a charming man from the Highways Department who was telling us how beautiful the Ardèche is and how lucky we were to have come here. We couldn't help but agree. Soon people began to leave. *"Allez, bonsoir, bon appétit!"* We went to our table and sat down to dinner.

"That couldn't have happened in England," said Alan. "That was really nice. I liked the chap from the Highways Department especially." We got to know this man, Fred Ode, much better later on, and his wife and daughter, and became very good friends.

There were a lot of people eating at the hotel, including the proprietor and his wife, who were sitting the other side of the room. The meal was simple but enjoyable, more so because we had a very pleasant musical background from a record player in the corner. Alan's a great jazz enthusiast and we were both very happy to listen to Teddy Wilson, Louis Armstrong, Duke Ellington and Ella Fitzgerald whilst we ate. When we were waiting for our coffee, the proprietor called out to us in English, "You like zis music, yes?"

"Very much," replied Alan. "I played jazz trumpet in a band in my youth."

"Come and have your coffee with us, and a brandy, then we can talk," said our latest new friend in French.

At midnight, many tracks and several brandies later, we were still there talking. Roger and Micheline told us they had bought the hotel two years before. They had renovated it and now had four bedrooms as well as the restaurant and bar. Their next project was to be a jazz club in the cellar.

As we drove up to the village at about 1am, we were very happy. Granted we'd consumed far more than our usual quota of alcohol, but we still felt that our warm glow was as much due to the friendliness of everyone we'd met as to the wine. As we breakfasted, hangoverless, on the terrace the next morning, we felt extremely pleased with life.

Our Sunday lunch did nothing to break the spell. We sat down to eat in the large Balazuc kitchen at 1pm with Geo, his wife, Jeanine, his mother, his father, his uncle, his brother, his two sons, Christian and Alain, and his six-year old daughter, Ghiselaine. We ate *pâté* and olives, asparagus with mayonnaise, followed by the traditional Easter dish of young roast kid. As usual, there was a salad after the roast, then happily a temporary break, though the wine continued to flow. Fresh goat cheeses and a huge apple tart were then placed on the table with some sparkling white wine to accompany them. Finally, by now groaning inwardly because of vastly overfull stomachs and light heads, we had cherries in brandy. Such a feast!

"These cherries are from your tree," Madame Balazuc told us. The most amazing thing about this meal was that nothing had been bought except the olives. The 1957 frost had killed off most of the trees. Throughout the three hours we were at the table, talk like the wine, flowed free. We discussed football, hunting, fishing, *boules*, politics, education, the Americans, World War II and the Resistance. Although this was a peasant family, they were lively, intelligent, well informed, had opinions on everything and a delightful sense of humour. They continually paused to check Alan was understanding everything.

Our next talk with Geo was about business. We paid him 3,441F (about £300) for the new roof. He promised to ask the carpenter to put in three new windows with shutters downstairs and to get the plumber to fit a sink in our dining kitchen and a shower and basin in the far room by the summer. He explained that I should have to wait for my WC until they'd demolished the old silkhouse, because of the drainage that would be required. He said he would work in conjunction with the others, making good all the plaster in the three downstairs rooms.

The night before we left, we sat making lists and doing sums.

"We couldn't have had a new roof in England for £300," Alan said. "5F an hour for a skilled workman is ridiculous!" It didn't seem too much, but I was very glad that the next bill would be for work in the part of the house we'd be living in. I should need another £300 at least before July.

That summer, we had to drive down through Germany, as Jan was exchanging with a German penfriend from Wiesbaden. We couldn't have found a more friendly household and spent a hugely enjoyable evening before leaving the next day for the Ardèche for the second time that year. It rained incessantly all the way and the roofrack was loaded with cupboard kits and chipboard. But we apparently wrapped it well enough and, as often happened, the sun came out to cheer us when we'd crossed the plateau and began to descend the Ardèche valley. I was so impatient to get there, to see if Geo had done the work he'd promised.

It was a close thing! The plaster was not yet dry in the kitchen, but it was all finished – sink, heater, basin, shower, windows and shutters. Triumphant, we could tackle anything; we had two weeks to finish our kitchen. There were shelves, cupboards and a bar to make, as well as the painting. We hoped the money would stretch to a fridge, but we had to pay the plumber and the electrician as well as Geo. The cupboards were not difficult to assemble, the shelves much more of a problem because no wall was straight. At last, with incredible patience, Alan had them all in place and started painting the walls before mounting the cupboards. The new rough plaster soaked up emulsion like a sponge. There was just enough for two coats and the transformation was amazing. It was the first colour in the house.

Then came a whole day spent laying the vinyl, struggling with the same problems – no straight walls, no right-angled corners – all in August temperatures. But again, the same reward. The cement floor disappeared and with it the prison cell feeling. The 3-burner cooker was fixed up at the side of the sink with its gas bottle underneath. Pans went on the shelf above and kitchen tools on hooks in the wall.

"Tomorrow I'll put the cupboards up over the bar," said Alan, "and then you can put all the china and stores away. It'll look proper posh!"

I'd brought a lot of crockery and was impatient to unpack it all. Whilst Alan had been working in the kitchen, I'd been trying to restore the quarry tiles in the middle room to a more presentable state. I've never been one for doing things the easy way; my kids have always teased me for it. I scraped, rubbed with steel wool and washed each tile three times. Huge drops of perspiration fell off the end of my nose as I worked in a bikini top and shorts, bruising and blistering my knees in the process. Then the joy of applying the polish. What a difference!

"I've finished," called Alan, just before lunch the next day. "The cupboards are up. We can unpack."

Delighted to see fresh, white cupboards, side by side, against the primrose walls, I started enthusiastically to unpack the boxes. Having put the cans, jars and packets in the first, I was just filling the second one with china, reaching up with the last soup plates in my hands, when the cupboard began to tip towards me, dragging the first one with it. Plates, cups and saucers cascaded out. As the doors of the stores cupboard opened, tea, coffee, rice, sugar, jam, flour and salt began to slide off the shelves and smash on top of the china debris already on the floor.

Alan came rushing in from the terrace to find me standing in this horrible mess with blood streaming down my face, hands and legs. There seemed to be nothing left whole except the soup plates in my hands. It was too much for me. I sat down on the floor and wept, still clutching my plates. When we'd wiped the blood and tears away, I realised I miraculously wasn't too badly hurt. The long bar underneath was still intact, anyway, the cupboards too. We even salvaged a few cups and saucers. It took us an hour to clear up and pull ourselves together.

"Well, we've had the lot now," I said, "blood, sweat and tears."

"How on earth am I going to fix those bloody things?" said Alan. He solved it in the end with much stronger rawlplugs and fastening the cupboards with chains to the beams.

"Belt and braces," he said, "they can't fall down now." And they haven't. When we came in later that night after eating out, it truly was a sweet pleasure to switch on the light (we had two now!) and look at our new kitchen.

We'd transformed the other rooms too. We now slept in the end room in our inherited mahogany bed with its new mattress. We'd bought a cheap, plastic wardrobe and put it across the room, so that this, with a curtain, divided off the basin and shower. At the bedroom end, we had a carpet (the floor was cement, not tiled, here), and more of the grey vinyl in the shower room. We'd painted the walls pale green in there and peachy beige elsewhere. It was a joy to be able to put our clothes away, to wash and shower in comfort, to have hot water, a working kitchen, to be surrounded by clean walls and look out of unbarred windows. What progress!

When Jan arrived after her stay in Wiesbaden, she was most impressed but grumbled that we'd left her nothing to do.

"Rubbish," said Alan. "You can paint the shutters. Both sides, two coats, three pairs!"

And she did. For the next three mornings, before it got too hot, she painted in her bikini on the terrace. Meanwhile, Alan painted the old front door as a temporary measure. We intended to have a new one made as soon as we could afford. I varnished all our new chestnut window frames. When it was all finished, we felt we shouldn't be too ashamed, when the old silkhouse was pulled down, to reveal the house to the village below.

The total bill was 4,000F for all the work. We paid the electrician 400F. After buying the vinyl and wardrobe, we had no money left for a fridge.

"Next year," I promised myself.

We made the most of the last few days of our holiday. We'd already taken Jan to Roger's club. It was too hot and crowded at weekends but other nights it was quieter and more intimate. We gradually began to get to know a small group of people who always spent their holidays in Joyeuse, friends of Roger from Paris, Nimes and Aix-en-Provence, but the most outstanding character was a maiden lady in her early 80s.

Hélène, Ardechoise born and bred, was a mine of information about everything and everybody in the region. She was very interested in the house and came up to see us one day on her moped! She was most insistent that we must renovate the old wing one day. We agreed but pointed out that we had to make the other side fit to live in first.

"It'll be some time before that side's habitable," I said sadly, as she stood on the rickety staircase peering upwards. Hélène told us it was 'la clède' (the local word for smoke room) and explained the process to us. The fireplace in the old kitchen had an open chimney. Above it there had once been a huge trough where tons of sweet chestnuts would be spread out, and the heat burst the husks off.

"What then?" I asked.

"Next time you come into Joyeuse, I'll show you the boots they wore to tread the chestnuts. They had long spikes on them. They trod the nuts into a paste in big tubs. The animals ate them, and us too when times were hard."

These chestnuts are still harvested in the Ardèche, eaten boiled with salt as an accompaniment to roast meat, wild boar particularly, or made into *purée* and *marrons glacés*, but the spiked boots aren't much in evidence these days!

It was Hélène, too, who suggested that we call the house "La Clède." So, that became our address: La Clède, Ribes, par

Joyeuse, Ardèche.

We felt we'd achieved a lot in 1965 what with a sound roof, new windows and a new kitchen and shower room. When I opened my Christmas present from Jan, I found a house sign, white on black. It has been hanging over the door for ten years now and reminds me always of that Christmas morning and my very great pleasure. Jan had a wonderful idea when she chose that present. Instead of an old ruin, we now had a house called La Clède.

CHAPTER 4

TERRACE WITH A VIEW

I f all the promised work had been completed during the winter, La Clède would have a long, south-facing terrace for us to sit on in 1966. Geo had agreed to begin the demolition. The carpenter had been asked to make us an open staircase leading up from the middle room, as well as windows and shutters for the upstairs granary. Geo had warned us that the carpenter had been known to keep people waiting for years, so we were prepared for some disappointments as we arrived in the Ardèche in Easter 1966. We were not, however, prepared for the weather. It was bitterly cold in Joyeuse and snow was falling gently. Alan parked the stationwagon in front of the Post Office.

"What's wrong," I asked. "I've bought bread and milk. There's nothing else we need."

"Sure?" asked Alan, as we sat looking at snowflakes melting on the car bonnet. "I think it might be a very good idea if we bought a fire."

"You're right. It'll be cold in the house. I hope we can find a cheap one."

We bought a gas bottle fire that had been reduced because it had a chip in it, piled it in the back amongst all the boxes and luggage and drove on up to Ribes. Not even the cold could chill my spirits as I got out of the car to admire our house, which we could see from the road for the first time.

"Well, there you are," said Alan. "Just look – and it's all yours!"

"I'm looking," I replied, "and the carpenter hasn't been. No windows upstairs."

But how different it was with the lean-to, the stone arch and the other derelict building gone. The foundations of the silk-house were still there, the steps up to the terrace were very battered and the extension of the terrace had still to be surfaced. The general effect was one very familiar to us – an uncleared bombsite!

Monsieur Toral, our neighbour, appeared on his terrace and of course we could now see him from ours. After greetings were exchanged, he said, "I thought we'd lose that at one stage," pointing to the curved wall of the old wing. "But it's still standing. I finished it yesterday."

The whole wall of the old wing had been repointed. The surface waved in and out visibly, but it looked solid enough.

"We'll be doing the other one later when we've finished the terrace."

"I see the carpenter didn't manage to get here then," I said, pointing to the existing shutters.

"Oh yes he did. He's made you a staircase, but you wouldn't believe the problems we had in there."

We couldn't wait to get inside and see. We had indeed now got a simple, open-tread staircase, and there was an Arctic blast of cold air coming right down it.

"Well, it did just cross my mind that it might be a bit draughty if the carpenter hadn't been," said Alan.

"Good on you for thinking of a fire. Let's get it in here before we freeze to the floor. I'll put the kettle on."

Throughout our stay that Easter we had a big struggle to keep warm. During the day we had bright sunshine and it was much warmer outside than in. After dark it was chilly. We put the gas fire in the end room so that at least we went to bed in comfort, but it was an ordeal getting up in the morning. In the kitchen we made huge wood fires – we had all the old roof timbers to burn. Sometimes, when the wind blew in the wrong direction, we nearly choked to death, but the fire was so cheery and welcoming.

Geo told us later that they'd had to move a beam in order to fit the staircase in and that the old silkhouse had stubbornly defied all their efforts to knock it down.

"We had to dynamite it in the end. The whole village showed up and cheered when the walls eventually fell!"

"What about the rest of it?" I asked tentatively.

"Oh, we'll do that we we've finished the terrace," he said, implying as always that there would be no problem!

"Before we come in the summer" I wheedled.

"*Oui, pas de problème.*"

And with that we had to be content. Alan's DIY job this mini-trip was to tile the shower. It would have been wiser to leave it until summer. Although we knew that the walls were uneven, he'd not realised the extent of the problem until he got going. It was his first attempt at tiling, and it quickly started to show! It was also extremely cold and uncomfortable, squatting in the shower tray and trying to cover bumps in the walls with 3" square pieces of ceramic. He was unfamiliar then with the French method of putting at least one inch of cement on the wall first before placing the tiles! I could hear the air turning blue, not only with the cold, but with his frustrated outbursts, and felt all I could do was bring in innumerable mugs of steaming coffee and keep the home fires burning! About every half hour or so, he'd come and stand with his back to it until he was practically scorching, in an attempt to warm his frozen bum!

It must be said it was not a job with which television's DIY expert Barry Bucknall would have been impressed, but we were mightily relieved when it was finished. We just didn't have enough tiles either, of course!

"It's fine, darling – who cares about the odd bump! It protects the walls and that's what matters. It's getting more homey all the time."

I was desperately trying to cheer him up as we sat on the terrace after lunch. Alan was not satisfied with his work and was feeling a bit down. We were just planning a shower to celebrate when we heard a car draw up nearby and English voices. Quite unexpectedly, some very old friends who'd been touring in the

Lot and Tarn valleys had turned up to inspect our ruin. They were themselves in the process of converting an old stable block in a village just outside Bristol and, of all our friends, they were the ones who were most sympathetic to our project.

We showed them round and discussed our various experiences and problems, and, God bless them, they made encouraging noises for once! They'd booked a room in Joyeuse and we arranged to meet them later at Roger's hotel for a drink before going out to dinner.

There were ten of us altogether that evening, sitting around a table in a restaurant of Roger's choosing. You can be almost 100% sure, when three or more French people are in this situation, that they will not only eat with relish but also talk quite a lot about food. They say of themselves that they think only of their stomachs. Though this is an exaggeration, it is definitely true that they have a very different attitude to food from the British. It is a sacrilege to them to regard it simply as fuel.

Obviously good cooking can be found in any country. Even the French acknowledge that some Chinese cuisine is excellent. What delights us are the particular blends of flavours, the fine sauces, the wonderful fruit and vegetables which are at the heart of French cooking. At the same time we're very aware, and not such besotted Francophiles, that we know it's possible to eat very badly in France. And on this particular evening we did. Roger was outraged! The staff may have been jaded after the Easter rush (the excuse given), but we were not at all happy with the very mediocre *gigot* of lamb, an extremely limited cheeseboard and the burned apple tart that we were offered that night. A great pity as the company was good and it was everyone's last night before leaving for their various main homes the next day.

We ourselves had one more day, but there was little else we could do until the summer. Even then we would be dependent on certain heavy work having been completed. Geo had promised me that I should sit on my new terrace before summer was over.

In July we celebrated our Silver Wedding anniversary. When people asked me what it felt like to have been married for twenty-five years, I could only say: "Surprised!" It was very difficult to realise that we'd reached this particular milestone, that we had a son just about to graduate and a daughter soon to go to university herself. We had to accept that, however young in heart we felt, we were in the most unexciting time known as middle age.

On the strength of Geo's promise, as one of our presents, we asked for and were given, a parasol and table and chairs for the new terrace. But promises, alas, are made to be broken. When we arrived that summer, it looked as if they'd started it the day before, which of course they had! The steel joists for the terrace were being laid, but apart from that, absolutely nothing had changed. I held back my disappointment, telling myself that at least they'd started. To my dismay, the next day at midday, Geo began to load up his lorry.

"Aren't you coming back this afternoon?" I asked sweetly.

"No, no more here this week. I have something else to finish first."

My heart sank. I was expecting a few guests soon and we'd be somewhat squashed just on the old terrace. Jan was at a summer school for two weeks but would be arriving later. I was also expecting my niece with a friend, as well as Ian on his way back from Spain. I set up the new parasol, table and chairs on what we had and hoped for the best.

It was rather a matter of chance when Ian would arrive. During the last four years I'd become accustomed to the casual arrangements of students. I was quite used to three or four friends joining Ian for his weekends home, all apparently in a state of semi-starvation. All these young people were very interesting to talk to because they made full use of their freedom. During their long summer vacations they roamed all over Europe with their student tickets, scooters, old bangers, or simply hitching lifts. They were prepared to work at fairly unpleasant jobs in order to achieve this. Ian had been a temporary postman, a Securicor guard, a motor-mower repairer and a waiter at Gatwick airport. Some of his friends had sold petrol or ice cream, moved furniture and driven lorries. I think all this made them more resourceful than we were at that age and very much at home in any company, but the biggest bonus was that they made a lot of friends from many different countries.

Oddly enough, Ian had a student friend, also called Ian Anderson and another Alan, like my husband. The three of them had just graduated together, all in modern languages. We were enjoying a drink back home after a swim in the river one morning when these two friends of Ian turned up, expecting to find him there with us. Two days later they left and shortly after Ian arrived, rather cross that he'd missed them. The day Ian reluctantly left in his turn, my niece Gill and her friend Penny arrived from Geneva. The day after came Jan.

Through all these visits we kept hoping to see Geo's face too, returning to finish the terrace, but nothing happened. We were so busy showing the Ardèche to our young visitors that I had little time to worry about it thankfully. But I was finding it a little difficult coping with hearty appetites on my small 3-burner cooker. I was very grateful for my new fridge, which had been delivered at the start of the holiday, but an oven would have been a boon.

When we were once again on our own, we were awakened one morning at 7am by noises and voices outside.

"Wake up, Al! The bloody builders are here," I yelled, opening the shutters.

At midday, they were just finishing the concreting. It was incredibly hot and they were working in full sunshine. We were just amazed that they'd carried on.

"Right, we're off now," said Geo. "You must throw buckets of water over it every hour or so or until the sun is off it. Otherwise it will crack. Tomorrow we'll come and do the steps and the posts and rails."

So, Alan and I took it in turns all afternoon, watching the shadow as it gradually covered the terrace. The next day we had to repeat the process with the steps. Only then did I have my new 'stage' on which to place my terrace furniture and my geranium pots. It was again very hot and impossible, even with the parasol, to eat out at midday, but in the evening it was wonderful. At 9pm the stones of the old walls were still warm. A slight breeze cooled us a little. We were celebrating with fillet steak, something I simply couldn't afford for more than the two of us. This dinner was very memorable, not so much for the food as for the magic of the night itself. The sky seemed vast and full of stars. There was a full moon, which bathed the countryside with a gorgeous light and coolth that was a relief after the intense sunlight during the day. Perhaps we lacked the sound of water lapping or trickling, but the continuous chirping of the *cigales* is also pleasant background music. We ate and felt like kings.

This was the first of many such evening meals – I simply hadn't realised what a pleasure it is to eat outside on a balmy evening and linger on afterwards with pleasantly full stomachs, the wine and conversation continuing to flow happily. We ate breakfast on the terrace too – it was in shade until about 10am. But it was too hot for lunch. The heat rebounded off the walls and concrete and made even a fervent sun-worshipper like me retreat into the shade. We would have to have some sort of frame built to bear a vine or creeper. Our new south-facing terrace was a little too hot for comfort.

When my sister, Sheila and her family called in on the way home from Spain, we were grateful that all seven of us were now able to spread out a little. Though Sheila saw that we'd already made a huge improvement to the old ruin she'd first seen, I think she was still rather dubious about the whole thing, and not altogether without cause.

In spite of the new steps and terrace, the whole place looked rather messy. The old kitchen still had its original door, window and shutters; the original main entrance door was only minimally improved by three coats of paint. One wall had been repointed but not the other. The first floor still had its old shutters, though windows now thankfully, and the courtyard, with the foundations of the old ruin showing, still looked like a bombsite. Never satisfied with what had been achieved, I wanted to do more, much more!

So, the next job was to get the yard cleared up. Geo had promised that he'd do this during the winter. He would repoint the other wing and suggested that, when he levelled out the courtyard, he'd build a ramp as a drive-in for the car. He gave me a rough estimate for this, and we calculated that, with what I'd already paid for (the first stage of the demolition and the terrace), the whole job would cost 4,000F. If you added this to the 3,500F we'd already spent on the roof, it came to about £500 to date. We'd have an open view, a large terrace and a drive-in.

But improvements were needed inside too. Unfortunately, another problem had arisen. Rain had started to come in through the roof in several places during the winter. This was due to broken tiles which had now been replaced, but enough damage had been done to necessitate new boards in several places. When we inspected these carefully, Alan reckoned that it wouldn't be good enough just to patch up in odd places.

"We really ought to refloor the whole granary."

"Must we?" I sighed, fearing it would cost a fortune in the first place and in the second that it would be too much for the carpenter. "He's got the shutters to do. He'll never do the floor as well!"

Alan persisted, and I gave in reluctantly, adding a new floor to the list of outstanding jobs to be paid for and crossing off new front door. Are carpenters the same the world over, notorious for delaying tactics?! Dédé Latour, though a delightful man, was one of the most casual about time we'd ever come across. We got all sorts of comments from the local people: Don't go to him if you're in a hurry. You'll die waiting for furniture – kept me waiting six years for a chest of drawers, etc, etc.

But it was not simply a question of a craftsman taking his

time. These men were busy. Like they'd never been before. We should have understood better that it would be increasingly difficult to get work done. All the local people, after years of putting up with their parents' style of living, were suddenly demanding a little more comfort and convenience. They were modernising their kitchens, putting in bathrooms and flush toilets, extra lighting and heating. I remember Roger saying to me once, "You know who'll be the richest people in the Ardèche over the next ten years? The plumbers, carpenters and electricians!" He certainly was right.

The other thing we didn't realise at the time was that we were at the forefront of a wave of people also looking for holiday homes. Some of the French friends we'd met at Roger's, who normally rented summer houses, were now looking for something to buy. Jean and Claude Caute from Paris came that year to look at a house which was for sale in Ribes. It was about half as big as La Clède and needed lots of work. The asking price was now £3,500. They came over to visit after they'd had a look at it, a bit disgusted and disappointed with the property they'd seen. It was the first time they'd been *chez nous* and they kept saying, "You were very lucky to buy when you did. Not only have prices gone up at least six times in the last three years, but old houses are becoming harder and harder to find. In pretty villages like this, people can ask ridiculous prices. Someone will buy that house within a month." It was sold two weeks later.

We were very heartened to hear all their comments, but it was obviously going to take us longer than we'd hoped to finish the house. We'd made a good start, however, and this year we felt we'd won something else which was beyond money and unplanned. We were beginning to feel very much part of the community. Our neighbours, the Torals and the Balazucs, the people in the café and in the baker knew us and our children. They had been delighted that all our young visitors had chatted to them in French. From that year onwards we were always asked if Jan or Ian would be coming.

Outside the village we had quite a large group of friends whom we should be seeing each summer for many years to come if they succeeded in finding properties. We were well known too in the shops in Joyeuse, as any foreigners would have been. We were the first English family to settle in the area, but most unexpectedly we now had a compatriot only a few miles away.

She was another Janet, a few years older than our own. We often ate in the evenings in a small, old-fashioned commercial hotel, in the next village Lablachère. The food was simple but well cooked and presented and excellent value. In 1966 it was 9F per head, wine included. As I couldn't make a meal at home for two for less than 10F, this was cheap indeed. We'd been sent there in the first place by the Balazucs. Madame Heyraud, the proprietress, had been brought up in our village and her son, Bernard, had trained as a chef in Nice and had worked for Trusthouse in England. He spoke excellent English and this year had brought home an English bride. He was now helping his mother to run the hotel.

Janet, his wife, arrived not knowing a word of French. She was lost at first and very pleased always to have a chat with us. Fortunately, she had a good ear and the sunniest disposition possible. After the first few difficult months she was able to help in the restaurant though it was a long road to complete fluency. Now, sadly, both Bernard's parents are dead, but Janet has two little girls who are completely bi-lingual.

In the village there was another little girl who had become a close friend – Ghiselaine, Geo's daughter. She loved to come to the house and hear me talk about school in England. Alan would sing English songs to her and practise his own French. Children are excellent teachers when you're trying to speak in another language, because they're so direct and have a limited vocabulary.

One morning, a few days before we were due to leave, she showed up at the house.

"Grandma says will you come to dinner tomorrow night.

She's going to do some rabbits, I think. I like it when you come because I expect Maman will make a tart for you."

We had a very small lunch because we knew we should have to stretch our appetites in the evening. Even so we were feeling very full by the time we'd eaten soup, *pâté, saucisson* and the rabbit cooked in wine. To our great surprise and dismay, Geo began to sharpen his carving knives when the rabbit casserole was cleared away. The next course was roast duckling! Alan continued manfully to the end but I had to slide my cherry tart on to Ghiselaine's plate. I'd had it. Where did they put it all?!

I asked Geo if he minded if we talked business for a while.

"Alan thinks we ought to have the whole of the granary refloored instead of just patched up. Do you think there is any chance that the carpenter will do it as well as the shutters?"

"I'll do my best to persuade him," he said, but I could see from the look on his face that he wasn't terribly hopeful this time.

"It's no good fretting about it," said Alan, trying to console me as we walked along the road back home. "If Geo gets the other work done, it'll be a big step forward. We might even begin to grow a few things round the courtyard once it's cleared."

This, as it was obviously meant to, cheered me up and distracted me. It would be wonderful to have a garden . . .

As I packed the bags this time, I wished, as always, that we could stay longer. I really felt that I should like a week's holiday without workmen at the house and without visitors. Even though we'd eaten out quite a lot, I'd done a lot of the cooking this year with rather inadequate equipment. We loved having our young folk and their friends, but it certainly was rather tiring. It would be simpler, of course, when we had a little more comfort – bedrooms upstairs, a proper bathroom – and a loo. Oh, for a proper loo! I just couldn't suppress my impatience to get on with the work.

Other people tell me that they're always pleased to get home from holiday. This was never true for me. It was not that I disliked my home in England or my job, but each year as we approached Boulogne or Calais, I was green with envy at the occupants of the GB cars driving south! As we drove on to the ferry, I would gladly have driven right round and off again. Once home, of course, I soon fell into the routine and rhythm of family life, though each year there were changes. Ian had no idea what he wanted to do except that he would prefer to work abroad. He took a temporary job until Christmas. Jan went off to university in Birmingham.

By new year 1967, Ian had saved enough money to set off on a European tour. For the first time for years, Alan and I were alone. The house seemed empty and quiet. Just before Easter when we were planning again to go to France, Alan's sister Molly died and all plans had to be changed. La Clède was forgotten as we sorted out family affairs. I found time to write to Geo and beg him to get on with the work even though we shouldn't arrive until July.

CHAPTER 5

THE BEGINNINGS
OF A GARDEN

Just after Easter, Ian arrived home; he has a habit of turning up unexpectedly. We'd had postcards from France, Italy, Switzerland and Germany since he left. The last news had been from Copenhagen about two weeks earlier.

"Where have you come from?" I asked as we all settled down to hear his news.

"I've hitchhiked from Hull," he said. "I docked there this morning from Sweden. I've got a job for the whole summer in the south of Spain, so I'll be off again soon."

"So you won't be coming to Ribes in the summer? What about you, Jan?"

She didn't know either. Eventually she decided to go to a summer school in Lyon for the first two weeks in July. In order to pick her up there, we decided to try a new approach to the Ardèche. We would put the car on the train ferry from Boulogne to Lyon. We'd often thought this might be a good idea if a little expensive.

But it's certainly the easiest and quickest way to get to La Clède. We left home in Surrey after an early lunch and were eating our next lunch on the terrace the following day, feeling comparatively fresh and relaxed.

We'd arrived in Boulogne about 6.30pm, had dinner and a stroll around before departure time at 9.15pm. The 2-berth compartment was small but it had its own basin and the bunks were comfortable. Alan was soon asleep. He's one of those lucky people who can switch off at will, which was a good thing as he'd been working very hard. I find it much more difficult to relax.

As we rattled along towards Paris, I was forward-planning as usual, wondering if we were going to be able to get the house finished by 1970. I'd not so far said very much to Alan but it seemed to me that the time had come to get rid of "Headingley," our large Edwardian house in Redhill, now that Ian and Jan were so rarely at home.

I remembered the day in 1959 when we first went to look at it and how I hadn't even wanted to get out of the car.

"It's hideous," I said. "I hate all those bays and gables."

It had reminded me of the first house we'd bought in Wimbledon ten years earlier. At that time, with property in short supply after the war, I'd been so pleased to get out of a 3-room flat that I hadn't cared about the outside appearance. I was just thankful to be able to spread a little with my two small children and their attendant clutter.

In 1952, after looking at seventy-six houses, we left Wimbledon and bought a very badly built modern house in a beautiful location at the foot of the North Downs. At first the children had been very happy at the village school, but by 1959 they were both travelling daily by train into the nearest town. It was time to move again and once more there was very little on the market. The "hideous" house was the fourth we'd come to view.

Eventually, Alan had persuaded me to look at it. There was a big garden and the house was solidly built with 100ft of frontage, but inside and out it seemed to be in the same state as when it was erected just before World War I. I'm sure the first owners were very proud of the lavatory in the downstairs cloakroom. It was a very shapely affair with blue flowers and bore the inscription 'The Original Burlington'.

The present owners, a middle-aged couple, had started decorating. The wife announced that they'd just finished the dining room as she proudly threw open the door. In our time we must have looked at over a hundred houses and been aghast at some of the rooms we'd seen. This dining room undoubtedly took the prize for the unexpected. Eight years later, as I lay on my bunk on the night train, I could still see it clearly. The floor was covered with a brightly patterned linoleum; the windows were curtained, as were all the rooms in the house, in flowered cretonne, mainly red and blue. The heavy, old, 4-panel door had been made flush with hardboard and had been painted yellow, as had the 18" skirting boards. The fireplace had been removed and replaced by an inset electric panel fire with a yellow tile surround. But it was the wallpaper which really defied belief. The design was of a series of jugs and plates arranged horizontally as if on shelves in every possible permutation of size, shape and colour, the whole bespattered with gilt. The walls were finished off with a frieze of blue flowers against a yellow picture rail. There was nothing in the room except a full-size table tennis table, a ball and two bats!

And we ended up buying it. It was enormous and terrific value for money, even though every room in the place would have to be redecorated. It took us five years to get it to our liking, by which time we'd become very fond of it. It was warm and spacious and a very practical family house. Though it was far too large for two, it would be a wrench to leave it.

The garden had always been too big – a problem for weekend only gardeners, which was all we had time for, since we both worked. In 1962, we'd sold a large piece of land at the side of it, and it was this money that bought La Clède.

"If I'd refused to go and look at that house," I thought in horror, "we shouldn't now be on our way to Lyon." I'd come round full circle and started wondering again if Geo would have done the work he'd promised.

I remember the train stopping in Paris but after that I must have dozed off. The next I knew it was 6.30am and we were pulling into Lyon station.

"If Geo has built the ramp," said Alan, as he turned the car out of the church square, "we should be able to drive straight up." Round the corner we went into the alley and, sure enough, up the ramp and into our own courtyard! We all jumped out (Jan was with us again) and immediately realised that the work had only just been started. The whole 3-storey wall was hidden by scaffolding. It was lunchtime so no-one was around, but it was quite obvious that the repointing had begun that morning and that we would be having company for several days.

Disappointment awaited us inside. The carpenter had done nothing.

"Still no shutters. I'm a bit annoyed with Dédé," I said to Geo when they returned in the afternoon.

"I'm none too pleased with him either," he replied. "I've been down there three times and each time he's promised to come the next day."

"Shall I go and see if I can persuade him?" I asked. Geo grinned. "You'll have a bit of a trip; he's gone to Lourdes."

"I hope he asks the Good Lord to help him work a bit faster," joked Alan, which when translated made them all chuckle.

"Well, I'm tired of waiting. I think we'll try and find some-one else."

So, that was my first job of the year. I always seemed to spend so much time chasing round after people and I had to do all the hassling and persuading because Alan's French wasn't yet good enough. I decided to wait until the repointing was fin-ished, which took three days.

"It's a shame," said Jan. "I could have painted them if Dédé had been. She looked around the courtyard. "I think I'll start a garden instead."

"Oh, yes, Jan!" I agreed enthusiastically. "Where to begin?" We looked round our stony, bare earth in front of the house. "It's a bit of a challenge!" Geo's brother, Serge, had scythed down all the brambles; there was a fig tree still thriving, though apparently growing out of rock, and a lilac bush on its last legs. We all stood in the courtyard and discussed a plan.

"How about something like this? Flower beds round the edges by the terrace walls and enough turning space for the car." Alan drew a curve from the bottom of the steps to the edge of the ramp with his foot. "This seems as good a starting point as any. If we plant a vine or a creeper, we can eventually train it over a frame to give us some shade on the terrace. And here," pointing to the other side of the steps," we could have another creeper and frame to make a carport."

"Who'll make frames do you think"? I made a mental note to ask Geo.

Early the next morning Jan started. When Madame Toral saw her digging, she came to chat and before long had promised to plant us some roses in the autumn. Her husband promised a vine. Madame Balazuc passed by and said she'd plant a mimosa. That's the way it is here. Thanks to these dear neighbours, today at La Clède we have extremely healthy creeper over the terrace and carport, rose bushes and two magnificent mimosas. (These had to be cut down ten years later – they'd grown so huge, they were going to be troublesome to walls and roof. We're still using it for firewood and have planted another higher up the garden. Ed)

Alan and I decided to inspect our land a little more carefully than we ever had before. It formed a large wedge with the base at the side of the house, rising steeply in three more terraces, the longer side parallel to the top road. Above the road were three more terraces which had probably once been planted with olive or fruit trees. All that remained was the lone cherry tree on the very top terrace. But at road level, there was a large stone *bassin*, filled by a spring, the house's original water supply. (We discovered at a much later date that this parcel of land was actually not included in the *Acte de Vente*. Anyone seen the films, *Jean de Florette* and *Manon des Sources*?! Ed).

Below road level, behind the house, was a quince tree overgrown with creeper (which eventually killed it). There were stone terrace walls but they were so hidden by brambles and old vines that it was impossible to see what state they were in. The one immediately behind the house, however, which held up the bank, had given up the struggle and was gradually falling into the ditch. The plumber had put up guttering and a downpipe on the back roof, but as the ditch filled up with stones, broken tiles, brambles and weeds, there would be bound to be some damp, even through the thick walls.

"I really ought to clear that out," said Alan, "but it's hopeless trying to do that sort of work in this heat. What I'll do is saturate it with weed killer so that at least it doesn't get any worse for now."

Jobs like this, that really needed to be done, were a constant source of worry and frustration, as help was so hard to get. We couldn't see any of the land behind the house from the terrace, so we just tried to forget about it!

We could only see the courtyard and the first level of land. But it was a joy to see the courtyard neat and tidy at last with our few flowerbeds and, looking beyond, our ancient, gnarled pear tree, where I'd tied my washing line, rising above the waist-high grass and weeds. There was no point tackling that lot for the few hot weeks we were there in August.

"But one day we'll do it, won't we Alan? We'll plant some new fruit trees and we'll have a veggie patch and more flowerbeds . . ."

"Yes, my love. We'll do it all eventually, but let's get the house finished first!"

So the next day we went to find a new carpenter.

Roger had recommended one who lived in a village on the way to Largentière – Laurac. We found the place quite easily on the edge of the road just outside the village. Roger had told us that the owner, who was now quite elderly, had had the good fortune to have four gifted sons, three of whom worked in the business. The general appearance of the works was very neat and tidy, a rare thing in the Ardèche. We were most impressed and when we went inside we couldn't believe our eyes. It was a beautifully equipped, modern workshop, buzzing with the whir of machinery making assorted doors and windows. The adjacent storeroom was filled with every conceivable kind of wood and synthetic timber.

Soon we were talking in a little side office to one of the sons, tall, handsome and smiling. We explained where we lived and what we needed, said that Roger Furon had recommended us to come and that Geo Balazuc was our builder.

"Could you ask Geo to meet me at your house tomorrow evening, so we can talk it through together?" said the young man.

"Oh yes, of course" I said, astonished that anyone would be willing these days to come within 24 hours and matching his apparent enthusiasm tenfold.

"Of course, I don't suppose for a minute he'll show up," I said as we left, trying to prepare myself for disappointment as usual.

"We'll see," said Alan. "This is the first business I've seen where it looked as if they mean business."

I was wrong; Alan right. Geo was ready and waiting, sipping a *pastis* at 6.30 the following evening when Jean Tourel showed up. They shook hands warmly, announcing to us that they were distant cousins. Apparently two generations back there was a marriage connection. As this seemed to be a good start, we decided to go for it and ask for the works!

A complete new floor upstairs, as well as shutters for all the windows; a new front door, and a new door, window and shutters for the old wing downstairs. "We just want a simple, ordinary door for the old wing, " said Alan to me, "but something rather nicer, perhaps in oak, for our main front door. What d'you think?"

As I was about to translate for Jean, he came out with almost the same ideas, adding that we could incorporate some glass panels to give a little more light in the kitchen.

"Yes, good idea," said Alan. "I'll have a go at designing one." After the measuring and notetaking, we all went along to Geo's for a drink. Jean promised to do an estimate and send it by post. This in itself was quite a surprise but when it arrived only two days later we were astounded.

We immediately set off for the workshop to say that we accepted the estimate for 2,700F and very much hoped he'd be able to do the work during the winter. A positive response – I really felt we'd fallen on our feet this time. It was nearly midday by the time all the business was over. Jean offered us a drink to seal the deal and we followed him into his house near by to be introduced to his very attractive wife. She was in the kitchen, an ultra modern, tailor-made affair with Formica worktops, stainless steel sink, washing machine, the lot (way ahead of its time). We had our drinks in the office which wouldn't have disgraced a large company, beautifully furnished in light wood, with custom-made desk, filing cabinet and so on. It's difficult to convey how impressive this was then. The Ardèche was a poor and backward region of France at that time. Our visits to the estate agent, the solicitor, the electricity office and other official places had done very little to change this image. It was a joy to find someone behaving in such a professional, businesslike way. It made such a difference to my stress levels, I could have hugged them!

"What a pity we didn't go to them sooner," I moaned as we got into the car afterwards. It was Alan's turn to be cautious.

"Wait until next year before you cheer. But they certainly seem efficient and the estimate's not at all bad, considering what we've asked for."

I certainly felt much more cheerful about our future plans. As I walked up the path from the baker each morning, I could now see my house and the terrace with its colourful parasol.

"Next year the new shutters will be there too," I thought, as I pulled off and ate a piece of the deliciously crusty loaf. Quite often I set off grumpily on this daily trek after my first cup of tea – Alan never wanted to go and always timed his ablutions accordingly. But as I got that first whiff of newly baked bread, I began to feel better. And climbing the steep hillside path back home, the sun already hot on my back, looking around at the ripening grapes in the neat vineyards, the brilliant blue sky overhead, I'd feel a happy glow inside. "I do love it here."

And there was Jan already in her bikini carrying out the breakfast tray to the terrace. There is something quite unique about the first cup of fresh coffee and still warm bread and *croissants* with butter and jam. It's thoughts of such things that keep me going through an English winter.

Rather surprisingly, for the first time that year, we didn't have clear blue skies all the time. I think we'd grown to expect almost perpetual sunshine and found it very strange that after a bright morning the sky would cloud over. There was hardly any rain but the evenings were decidedly cool. For the first time we had a strong north wind – not the full force of the *mistral* (which apparently can drive people living in its path almost mad) - but quite unpleasant.

The local people were full of grumbles, prophesying a poor grape harvest. The peach crop was not as good as usual, they said, but they still tasted wonderful to us and were ridiculously cheap. Other food seemed quite dear. The exchange rate was much lower this year so I had to be even more careful than usual with meat and butter, for example. I'd discovered several things which it was advantageous to bring from England.

This food parcel contained: marmalade, jam, icing sugar, ground almonds, dried fruit, biscuits, cereals and tinned butter. I also packed detergents, soapflakes, washing up liquid and everyday medicines and toiletries, all of which were either unavailable then or cost the earth. Chemists are expensive places everywhere but try to avoid them in France at all costs. You'll never find a poor chemist!

People often ask me about housekeeping in France. In general, it is considered a very expensive place to spend a holiday. This is true on the tourist beat where a cup of tea and a Coke in a café are more than double the price in England. Convenience and frozen foods were rather rare in France in the sixties and not popular. Consequently, they were expensive and not considered everyday fare. (There's now a MacDonalds in Aubenas and it's particularly popular with the young, of course. Ed)

Our normal routine in August was to have a continental breakfast on the terrace after a wake-up cup of tea. The time varied between eight and ten, depending on the night before. Lunch also was a very elastic meal (compared with the sacred hours midday to two kept by the French), depending what chores we were doing. This was almost invariably salad, followed by cheese and fruit. For our main evening fare, we had a larger meal, usually four courses, like the French. Local chickens and rabbits bought from neighbours were cheaper than the butcher.

Over the years with inflation in France and the fall in the exchange rate, things have become increasingly dearer. We combat this by taking more food with us, eating out less often and latterly we've also grown our own vegetables. In the "summer of love" - 1967 – we had no inkling of these troubles in store but we did realise that the sooner we finished the house the better. We very much hoped that our new carpenter would help us more quickly on our way. We'd just been hearing more frustrating tales about the village carpenter from a new friend.

The year before, when we had no ramp up to the courtyard, a gentleman had appeared on the terrace, introduced himself in English and asked if we thought we'd have sufficient room to bring up our car. In appearance he was very French but we soon discovered that his mother was English, born in Northampton. As a boy he'd often visited relatives there but had lost touch since the war. His English was good and Alan was naturally pleased to make this contact.

Maurice and his wife rented a neighbouring house as a holiday home and he'd been considering buying a house there for many years. He often came to chat and in 1967, just before we left, he came to tell us that he was negotiating for a house in the village. He went on, "Of course, I was very angry with you when you bought this house! It was completely my fault, but I was cross just the same."

"What do you mean?" we asked puzzled.

"Well, as you know it was empty for six or seven years and each year I came to look at it but there seemed so much to do and there is so much land. In September '63 I decided to take the plunge and was completely overcome when the agent in Vals told me it was sold."

"Do you mean that if you'd gone a couple of weeks earlier that we should never have seen it?!" I asked amazed at the coincidence.

"Absolutely, but now I don't mind because I've found another one," he replied.

"And we should have bought the house at Fons," I said to Alan. "I'm so glad you pontificated, Maurice. I just can't believe now that Ribes would not have been part of my life. What a stroke of luck!"

When we went to see what he hoped to buy, we were rather surprised because it really was a complete ruin – trees were growing through the roof.

"Basically, I've bought the site and the stones," said our new friend. "I want to build a new house."

Certainly the site was one of the most beautiful in the whole village. From his living room window he would have a permanent view of the valley in almost the exact spot where Alan and I had stood entranced those years ago. As he hoped to live in the village all the year once he'd retired from his job with Renault in Paris, he intended to install central heating.

"He'll need it too, you know," said Alan, as we walked back to La Clède. "It faces almost due north." Remembering that bitterly cold Easter, I couldn't help but agree. The following day we saw another house which, though idyllic in summer, would not be a very comfortable winter home.

For quite some time, our dear friend Hélène had been urging us to go on a trip to see a monastery called Notre Dame des Neiges. We were interested enough because we'd read Travels with a Donkey and remembered this as a place where Stevenson had stayed. The monks were also reported to make excellent wine. Usually, we avoided long car trips in the August heat but as it was much cooler this year we finally arranged a date.

It was a lovely drive, the road rising through villages, vine-yards and forests until it crossed a high plateau with fold after fold of mountains stretching away into the distance.

But I've never seen anything less like a monastery. I suppose I was expecting cloisters and tranquillity. Instead the carpark was jammed and there were queues everywhere to go into huge modern buildings to buy wine, icecream, postcards and use the loos. We immediately turned round and left.

"We'll go see the dam instead," said Hélène. "Then, I'd like to call on a friend and introduce you." She didn't mention that the friend lived in a small *château*, beautifully situated on a small promontory in a natural lake.

It was quite breathtaking, exactly like the princess' castle in a fairy tale. After being shown round, we were invited to have tea. The woman's husband was an antique dealer who'd searched France to find exactly the right pieces for the lovely room we were in. Surrounded on three sides by water, we sat on a window ledge cut into the 3ft-thick stone walls and watched the lake lapping below us as the afternoon sun gleamed through the pine forest and sparkled on the water. We took in the beautiful Aubusson carpets on the stone-flagged floor, the magnificent chestnut tables, the settle and tapestry-covered stools and chairs. Such elegance. We had lemon tea and almond biscuits. How the other half lives.

"Rather nicer than the caff on Brighton pier," Alan whispered. I had to hide my smiles; it would have been lost in translation!

"Of course," said Hélène, as we drove down the Chassesac valley, "they close the house up in the winter. It's too cold. They have a lovely modern apartment in Paris."

La Clède looked very ordinary and uncomfortable by comparison. But I was not too downhearted because next year not only did we hope to have further improvements, but we intended to bring some antique furniture of our own. We'd inherited some rather nice old family pieces from my sister-in-law Molly's cottage which would fit in extremely well.

In the autumn, we sold the large house in Redhill and bought a smaller, modern one in Weybridge, complete with built-in storage. How to transport everything to France? Plans were laid for Operation Furniture Removal in Easter '68.

1964: Peg on terrace looking towards what will disappear

1964: Jan on precariously covered terrace

A

Easter 1965: View from front with silkhouse still in place

View from rear

*Above and below: Easter 1966: Silkhouse, etc demolished;
foundations remain*

Easter 1966: Peg and Al

Easter 1966: View from front with silkhouse and lean-to gone

Summer 1966: Work in progress on terrace extension

Summer 1966: Serge, left; Geo, right

E

1967: Completed terrace, steps, pointing, but still no garden

1969: Neighbour extends upwards, changing our roofline

F

1975: Peg dwarfed, and old wing hidden, by monster mimosas

As above.

G

Late '70s: La Clède much as it is today, with (below) new rear terrace

CHAPTER 6

ANCIENT AND MODERN
CONVENIENCES

I t cost us £18 to move our furniture from our new house to
La Clède, less than half what it cost to move from Redhill
to Weybridge. We hired a Ford Transit van for ten days
with insurance and permission to drive abroad. Actually, it cost
more than that door to door with petrol, etc. But, given that we
should have made the trip anyway in our own stationwagon,
the hiring of the van only put this small extra expense on the
bill. Can you imagine the cost today? (Three English builders
came over in 1995 in a hired – somewhat bigger – van full of
materials to redo the roof. The van hire cost about £800 for
three weeks. Ed)

The main problem was that we couldn't have the van until
the evening before our departure. So, although we could estimate what we could pack into it, we couldn't know exactly
what it would hold until we started loading. In the garage
we'd assembled two wing chairs, an oak blanket chest, a dresser, a corner cupboard, a chest of drawers, a gate-legged table,
an old kitchen cabinet, a bedside cupboard, a carpet, two cane
bedroom chairs and a coffee table. There was also a grandfather clock standing in the hall, but we weren't very hopeful of
taking it on this trip.

We got it all in, except the clock! We even managed to put the
best pieces in the middle with the worn out covers of the wing
chairs and the flaking paint of the kitchen cabinet very visible
at the back! We were very unsure of our reception at the French
customs. At the last minute I put the latest paid rates demand
for La Clède into my bag. It saved the day, I think.

At Boulogne I gave my sunniest smile. I said we'd been renovating a holiday house in the Ardèche and at last it was ready to furnish.

"We were horrified at the price quoted by removal firms," I explained, "especially as this is only surplus furniture, well used and worth very little. Are we breaking any regulations by bringing it ourselves?" I've found in these sorts of situations where one has to deal with officialdom, it pays to look very innocent and ask them for their advice. You thereby distract them from their main purpose which is to get you! I was just praying it would work this time.

The officer didn't reply. He started poking about in the back of the van. I showed him the rates bill. He still didn't say anything and went off the find a colleague. My heart sank.

They discussed the situation, poked about some more. The new man asked to see my bill and said authoritatively "You realise, Madame, that you are not allowed to sell any of this furniture."

I assured him this was not my intention. "It's from my home in England which I'm going to put in my French house. Afterwards, we'll buy what we need in France. I've already bought a cooker and fridge here." The two officials turned their backs and talked some more.

"What d'you think?" Alan whispered. "Well done, love, that last bit was good." I shrugged. I was quite prepared by now to have to unload the whole lot.

Then suddenly the second officer turned, saluted and said "That's all, Madame. You have chosen a beautiful region. I have a cousin in Privas." And to Alan, who'd just climbed back into the van, eager to be on our way, "Drive carefully, Monsieur."

Gleefully we drove down the ramp and along the quay. We intended spending our first night in an hotel about two hours' drive away. It was a lovely evening and we felt very light-hearted at having got everything through without any problems or cost.

Obviously, we had no museum pieces. Nevertheless, some

of the things were quite old and quite good country antiques.

"I do hope this is a good omen," I said. "This year's going to be a really good year, with all the work done and everything going smoothly."

And looking back, it was a good year, one in which we began to feel really optimistic about finishing the work in 1970 as planned. The second piece of good fortune, which was a change from our Easter visit of two years before, was the weather which greeted us. It was warm and sunny.

As we heaved and sweated, lifting the furniture up the steps and into the house, I realised that we couldn't have done this without the drive-up, nor would it have been very easy in the rain. Our third and biggest thrill was our beautiful oak front door. We had lots of opportunity to inspect it as we went in with furniture and out again to reload at the van. We must have made twenty trips. The rest of the work was done as promised – new shutters and door for the old kitchen and a complete new granary floor. The joy of this was that at ground level you looked up to a pine strip ceiling. "Won't it look great when we get the beams sanded?" I said, already planning more jobs.

Alan looked resigned. "I'm not looking forward to that much."

There had to be one disappointment. The wretched old shutters were still in place upstairs.

"I'll go and see him tomorrow," I said, feeling totally positive for once. "Perhaps he'll do them before the summer."

" I wonder if there's any chance of Geo doing the septic tank before then, mused Alan. (It was his job to empty the Elsan).

"That's too much to hope for, I guess, but wouldn't it be great?" I said. "I'm going to ask him. I'll get down on my knees if I have to!"

We worked for 12 hours the next day arranging the furniture and had no time to go to Laurac. The result of our day's work meant convenience instead of make-do and a little comfort at last.

For the first time we had adequate storage space. In the bedroom we had the chest of drawers. What joy to be able to unpack our suitcases completely and either hang or store away all our clothes.

We gained two things in the kitchen: more work surface and more cupboard and drawer space. As we passed through Joyeuse, we'd called in at Vedel and asked them to send up our new cooker, ordered the previous year. It arrived as we were rearranging the kitchen.

In France all cookers have a lid which provides a table top when the cooker's not in use. When it was in position between the sink and the fridge, I had a flat surface to work on. As I could quite often manage with the old 3-burner cooker, the new one was used mainly when I had guests. There was also a cupboard at the side of the oven to hold the gas bottle which made the whole thing very neat and compact.

The old kitchen cabinet has two drawers as well as cupboards and a drop-down table which was another very useful surface. When we painted it white it blended in fine with our other cupboards. It was certainly starting to look more together.

We turned our attention to the fireplace which we considered a bit of an eyesore as only the hearth was stone. We'd even considered pulling it out but had been so grateful for our wood fire when it was cold that we decided to keep it and make the best we could of it. I cleaned it out leaving the flat stone hearth quite bare. I bought the biggest earthenware pot I could find and filled it with a huge display of dried flowers and grasses, and made a pile of pine cones in one corner.

We'd also inherited some genuine horse brasses, which Alan's mother had collected, a pair of leather bellows, a long brass toasting fork and some pretty Spode plates. When these were all arranged, the fireplace became quite a pleasant focal point in spite of its obvious amateurish construction, and the whole kitchen looked more attractive and inviting.

Though the kitchen and bedroom were both improved, it

was the middle room which gained most from our vanload. Not until we were sitting drinking coffee after lunch the next day did we realise how much we'd missed having a really comfortable chair to sit in. We'd bought green loose covers for our wing chairs. The pale green carpet looked almost new too after a good shampoo and gave me six square yards less of red quarry tiles to polish! Just these two additions banished the air of make-do. But it was the old dark oak furniture, the dresser, chest and corner cupboard that really made the room like home, as well as providing us with more storage.

I had drawers for cutlery and table linen. Bedlinen for the divans went in the chest. For the first time I could display pretty as well as useful things in the glass-fronted corner cupboard. On the dresser we had two mahogany tea caddies and a battered and treasured Chippendale tray. When everything was arranged, we were so carried away we even hung up a few watercolours!

It was much less cold that Easter. We'd arrived on Good Friday in brilliant sunshine but two days later it was pouring with rain and it went on raining heavily for three days with only a few dry intervals. We felt trapped but at least it was now more pleasant inside.

On Easter Monday we were planning to go out to dinner with the usual group of friends. We left with umbrellas, dodging the waterfall cascading off the roof and the pools on the terrace and ran down to the road where we'd left the van. Unfortunately, Alan had parked off the tarmac and the van wouldn't move, the wheels spinning wildly and sinking deeper and deeper into the mud.

Before long Geo was there to see if he could help. He went to get his car and a tow rope. It was immediately obvious that the van was too heavy (even minus load) and that a tractor was the answer. But the tractor refused to start! By this time our neighbour and Geo's son Christian had also arrived – this kind of situation tends to attract a crowd – and all three were bending over the tractor engine in their shirts and jeans with the torrential rain beating down on them, whilst a group of wives and children stood watching the entertainment from under their big umbrellas. We stood helplessly under ours feeling extremely guilty for being the cause of all this trouble. At last the tractor engine fired, the rope was attached and in a matter of seconds we were hauled on to the road. There was a loud cheer from the assembled audience and broad grins from the three saviours who were by now soaked to the skin. I apologised profusely, but the response was only glee and "No need for showers now!" - so good humoured and good natured. One almost felt they had enjoyed the 'challenge'. (This unfailing helpfulness seems to have disappeared here far less than in other places and other countries; a natural kindness and pleasantness still abounds. Ed)

Our destination was a restaurant in the market square in Joyeuse which had been taken over by our friend, Fred Ode and his wife. We expected to find everyone already halfway through the meal – we were 45 minutes late. We should have known better – very little starts on time in France. The company was just assembling, chatting over *apéritifs*, and our late appearance was unsensational, though they enjoyed the story!

My main memory of that evening is of a young friend of Roger's who was working at the time as a rep for a cigar firm. At the end of the meal he produced a magnificent sample case. The evening ended in a cloud of fragrant cigar smoke and brandy.

This young man had just wrecked his car in his eleventh accident, which perhaps calls for a brief comment on French driving. There is 300% more road than in England and approximately the same number of vehicles, but there are nearly twice the number of accidents. Everybody drives very fast and the fact that almost all males consume 'some' alcohol every day may also have some bearing.

In sparsely populated country areas like ours, pedestrians do not seem to expect cars on the road and can be a positive danger. When the peasant farmers become drivers – and by

1968 they almost all had cars – they seem to think they still have the road to themselves.

We have often avoided contact by a hair's breadth as some old car has shot out of a field on to the road. These country folk, and many townspeople too, are very lax about having their cars serviced. To this day there is no MOT testing in France, so poor brakes, defective lighting and worn tyres are commonplace. So far we have survived unscathed though many of our friends have been in trouble more than once. (Tests have now been introduced. Ed).

In 1968 there was comparatively little traffic in and around our village. Each year the number of cars has increased and it pays to be extra vigilant, particularly on hairpin bends, since local drivers almost without exception prefer to drive in the middle of the road! These are kept in excellent repair – amazing considering just how many kilometres of road there are. Every year improvements are made, tracks tarred and gravelled, roads widened.

On the day the rain stopped, we went off to Laurac to pay our bill. Again we were invited in for a drink but we couldn't persuade Jean to come and do the upstairs shutters before July.

"I'm so very busy, but I do promise to come up in July to discuss the beginning of the whole upstairs conversion with Geo. We can do the shutters when we start work there."

"Well, I suppose that's better than nothing," I said, but we went off a little fearfully to ask Geo if he could possibly do the septic tank and the lavatory before the summer.

"That depends on the plumber" was his reply.

"But if he agrees, you'll do it?" I pressed him.

"Oh yes, it's not a lot of work."

As we had every confidence in our handsome young plumber, we counted that a firm promise.

"You'd rather have a loo than new shutters, wouldn't you," asked Alan. "I know I would." And on the last day of this trip, as he was carrying that dreadful Elsan over to the garden to empty it, he was singing the latest Stones single: "This could be the last time, this could be the last time!"

On this happy note we left for England.

There was a letter from Canada waiting for us. Ian had decided in March to go to Toronto where he had an old school friend. He'd found a job in a language school and was writing to tell us that he'd been awarded a student fellowship at Wisconsin University in October. He wanted to do a course in South American studies for his MA. This was good news. The next day Jan passed her driving test and was able to take herself back to Birmingham for the summer term in the little Minivan that Ian had left behind.

On 19 June we received a letter from Ian now in Mexico. It began:-

"I arrived here today after spending a week in New York and two days in New Orléans. I couldn't face a North American winter and intend to do my course here. The lectures will be in Spanish which I shall prefer. I stayed with Tom and Molly in New York, which was just like it's supposed to be, unbearably muggy. I was going to fly direct to Mexico City, but decided to go to New Orléans, at no extra cost, back to the source of "all that jazz." If I complained about New York, I just didn't know what was waiting for me down in the Mississippi Delta – 80°F at 10 at night and 85% humidity. Now you can understand The Blues but how the hell did they find the energy to sing and play?! I had a room in the old quarter and wandered down Bourbon Street and Canal Street where all the nightclubs blare out Dixieland. I took a ride on a mock paddle steamer, very touristy, but somehow unreal to look out of the air-conditioned cabin at the rotting swamp with an occasional glimpse through the foliage of a decrepit wooden cabin and an old negro sitting fishing on the water's edge.

"First impressions of Mexico City are of noise and too many *gringos*. I want to stay away from English-speaking people as much as possible. The city is enormous (about 7m inhabitants) and steadily growing. It's ringed by mountains, two of them snow-capped. It rains every day at 5pm. Traffic is suicidally crazy, with the small 15-year-old buses, bursting at the windows with people, weaving in and out like sports cars. The place is bustling with construction sites, including a metro, which is half completed and runs like a huge open ditch through the middle of the city. . . The letter concluded: It's nearly 8 o'clock and time for my *tortillas* and beans again (the food isn't too *cordon bleu* around here). Will write again soon if I don't get chilli poisoning. Ian. PS: Could you please renew my driving licence."

I think we were both a little envious. Alan would have liked very much to see the source of "all that jazz," but above all to be in Mexico City for the 1968 Olympics. Twenty years before, in 1948, he'd enjoyed every minute of the first post-war Olympics at Wembley, and would gladly have joined Ian in Mexico. Instead we took the familiar road to Dover, just the two of us. Jan was planning to drive down later with a friend.

We were fairly confident this year that the work would be done as promised and were looking forward to planning the granary conversion. We'd been let down before though and I didn't really believe it until I actually saw my latest mod con shining white and immaculate. I hadn't thought that I should ever look at a simple lavatory with such an idiotic smile on my face, but I found myself almost kissing it!

The bill for the septic tank, the loo and the plumbing was £80. This small sum can only be explained by the fact that the regulations in France did not specify that the tank be underground. Ours was tucked away in one corner of the cellar. (It has performed magnificently and almost odour-free ever since! Ed)

Our holiday had started on a happy note. We unloaded, delighted to take the dust sheets off the furniture and unpack our clothes. After showering and changing, we went down to La Récluse to find our friends.

Roger was sitting outside the hotel dressed as a Normandy peasant.

"I'm glad you're here. Jean and Claude are having a party.

They'll be cross if I don't take you along. Try to look like peasants!"

It turned out to be a housewarming, an inappropriate term as the temperature stayed in the eighties until well after midnight. The house, which they'd eventually bought after a two-year search was on the opposite side of the valley from Ribes in a small hamlet called La Crotte (this means turd!). The view from their small garden was spectacular. You could see the Ribes church tower high on the hill on the other side of La Beaume with the mountains behind. Originally there had been a monastery on the site. The land fell down almost sheer to the road below. At this point there was a large loop in the river and the valley was a geometric pattern of vineyards and orchards.

The party was held in the courtyard and a barbecue had been set up on the terrace. A cask of red wine replaced the English barrel of beer. Jean and Roger had fixed up lights and hi-fi equipment. A buffet table was laden with *pâtés*, cheeses, huge tarts and enormous baskets of bread and fruit.

We ate, drank and danced until midnight, when one of the guests made a speech welcoming the family to the Ardèche and wishing them health and happiness in their new home.

The Mediterranean climate is reliable enough to plan and hold outdoor events of this kind and for English people so used to being "rained off," it's an absolute joy. Throughout the whole of that August we had the most wonderful weather.

As we were so frequently invited out by other friends, we felt it was time to give a party ourselves. Even though the house was much more civilised, I didn't feel we were ready to have a party there, so we went up to our favourite mountain inn at Sanilhac.

I asked Madame Belin what she could provide for fourteen people.

"Whatever you like, Madame."

"Well, I'd really like fish to start rather than *pâté* and *charcuterie*, and if you could make us some tarts to finish, I should like that. Apart from those two things, I leave it up to you."

We were all assembled two evenings later in a large private room and began eating at 9pm. We started with eggs in a potato pancake. Then came the fish – trout with almonds. The main course was a leg of lamb, properly cooked, ie pink not raw, beans from the garden and *sauté* potatoes. As is usual in France, this was followed by a green dressed salad and cheese. All this was liberally washed down with local red wine. Apple tarts and coffee were served at 11pm. It was a beautifully cooked and presented meal. The bill was a little over £18.

This lovely mountain restaurant is closed now. Even if it were open we couldn't afford to give a party there. It would cost five times that, possibly more with our low exchange rate. We're so grateful we could do it then, that we could have such a wonderful evening for such a reasonable sum.

During the last week of that holiday I managed to get Jean and Geo together at the house. Geo seemed very reluctant to commit himself even though it was Jean the carpenter who had the major work to do.

For him there was a new ceiling, an area of about 600sq ft. I wanted the beams left exposed so that it had to be level in the centre and sloping at the sides. The windows and shutters were still to be done too, of course. Geo's job was to plaster the walls. I left them trying to sort out a mutually satisfactory date.

Jean said he'd send the estimate to England.

"What else can I say to spur Geo on?" I asked Alan.

"Nothing. Don't worry. When we get the estimate, we'll write again to Geo."

At that time we were still hoping to retire in 1970. We'd made good progress downstairs; now we needed to get the upstairs started. We needed another good year, but things didn't go smoothly for us, or for Ian.

CHAPTER 7

A SET-BACK OR TWO

Trouble started first for Ian far away in Mexico City. Many people will remember the student riots and near revolution which broke out in many parts of the world, but in Mexico too just before the 1968 Olympic Games. Apparently, the unrest started at the end of July; the whole university came out on strike. By September the strike was still not settled. This was Ian's letter of 19 September 1968.

"Today the army invaded the university and arrested 300 people, including the student leaders of the strike committee. The Government hopes that this will mean a return to classes next week at the latest, but if I'm judging the situation correctly there will be more barricades in the streets tonight, more fighting and more deaths. The Government is embarrassed by student demands to release political prisoners and by their protests against the corruption which runs right through the administration."

As the opening date for the Olympics approached, the Government obviously panicked. On television newsreels we saw the army machine-gunning the students and were naturally very relieved to get Ian's next letter dated 10 October.

"Official figures gave the results of the pitched battle as 48 dead, 500 wounded and 2,500 detained, but the Government has agreed to negotiate with the students which was all they were asking in the first instance. All this could have been avoided."

On 2 November Ian was told that courses would not be resumed until February. He couldn't afford to wait without a job but couldn't get a work permit without bribing several officials. He had to leave having lost all the fees he'd paid.

His next letter dated 8 December came from New York again where he was working as a waiter.

"New York is a frightening city, not only because it's so fast and so big but because of the friction resulting from people of different racial groups living elbow to elbow in conditions that don't make for gracious living. It's a young people's city too. Anyone who doesn't have to work here and has the money moves out. There are plenty of broken down old men, derelicts and alcoholics, who just seem to have been worn out by the struggle. This tension I feel is at the same time exciting. I'll maybe stay awhile though I don't think I'll be able to stand waiting at table for long."

This time we were not envious. One place I am not anxious to visit is New York. Jan, on the other hand, would have gladly taken the next plane, had her finals not been six months ahead. On a trip to Canada recently she did a side trip of five days in New York and, like Ian, found it very stimulating.

On Christmas morning the doorbell rang. There was Ian, looking rather thin and pale, but grinning broadly and saying "Happy Christmas," as I hugged him.

"Why did you come back this time?" I asked.

"I thought I'd like to see spring in England this year," he said.

"I sent a card to New York but no present," I said as we went inside. "I had a feeling you might turn up!"

I had, of course, sent my usual Christmas greetings to our friends in Ribes and Joyeuse. They returned their good wishes in the New Year but there was no mention of work done. Nor had we received the expected estimate from Jean.

"They must just be too busy," I said to Alan. "We'll turn up at Easter and find out what's happening."

All was quiet and calm, both in the village and at La Clède. It was always a joy to drive up the twisting road to the church, past the impeccably maintained vineyards and up the ramp into the courtyard. Over the years we'd noticed several new houses being built. There were now perhaps seven or eight in all, some of which we passed on the drive up. As we expected, no work had been done on the house.

The schools were closed for the Easter holiday and Ghiselaine, Geo's daughter, came running to say hello when she saw the car.

"I was waiting for Daddy," she said after the customary three kisses.

"Is he working in the village?" I asked.

"Yes, he's building the new house. They started last week."

I looked in despair at Alan. We'd been told this would be happening in the autumn.

"Come and help us unpack," I said. She was always fascinated by the things we brought from England. I usually managed to find a space for a game or a few sweets for her and the twin brothers she now had, Eric and Joel. They had arrived, rather unexpectedly, two years ago and were "devils" according to her mother, Jeanine. That made ten to feed each day in the Balazuc household – age range 2 to 88!

When Geo's lorry went past, Ghiselaine shot off to show her present. Five minutes later she was back with a huge bundle of asparagus and an invitation to go for a drink that evening.

"How can I go and start grumbling?" I laughed to Alan as I washed the asparagus, "when they're always so kind. And anyway, I suppose there's really no reason why we should have priority."

"If it rains he might come to work inside," said Alan. "That's our only hope."

That evening Geo confirmed this but insisted that the house must be his first concern. With this news we went off to Laurac to tackle the carpenter. For the first time I felt a little coolness in the usual polite reception. When Jean got his copy of the estimate out of his file, we understood why.

"But, I'm sorry, we never received it," I said in frustration. "You sent it to our old address." I thought I'd given him the new one. I could have kicked myself for not writing to check. We looked quickly through the estimate.

"Is there any chance of your doing it before July?"

"Yes, but I must have the plastering done first.

The best we could suggest was that he should get in touch with Geo if there were several days of rain.

"Surely we can get someone else to do the plastering," I said. "Let's ask everybody if there's someone they can recommend."

We went to see our friend, Maurice, who, though he'd retired and sold his flat in Paris, was still in his rented house. His new house was far from ready.

"Only by being here on the spot," he said, "shall I have any chance of moving in in the autumn. I spend all my time nagging people."

Our friends, Jean and Claude, were equally despondent. They'd combed the area trying to persuade builders, carpenters and gardeners to help them at their house. The friends from Brittany, Raymond and Evelyne, had given up altogether and planned to do everything themselves! Only André and Raymonde, some friends in Joyeuse, seemed to be making any headway. They couldn't find local workmen and were importing from Aix en Provence where they had their winter home and were giving them board and lodging as well as wages.

This was obviously a solution we could neither contemplate nor afford from a distance of 800 miles. What to do? Where to turn? We felt completely frustrated. Our five-year plan would break down if we lost a whole year. We'd hoped to pay our last bill in 1970.

In desperation we asked our neighbour, Monsieur Toral, if he could possibly do the plastering for us on his own. He too refused because he had too much to do in his own house. Madame Toral then told us that they planned to sell the half of the house they were living in and move into the other part round the corner. Her husband's first job would be to build a large terrace.

"You'll still be here in summer though, won't you?" I asked.

"Oh yes, but we shall put the house up for sale in July."

Although they'd been our neighbours for four years, the

house across from us was very little changed. Besides working quite often with Geo, Monsieur Toral had peach groves and vines to tend as well as his large garden. They had no hot water, lavatory or kitchen sink, except the original stone one. Madame Toral still cooked the most wonderful food on her wood-burning stove. I'd already realised that they must have borrowed the bulk of the £1,000 they'd paid for the house and had been struggling to pay it off. One son was still at home. All the other married ones left their children with her for part of the long summer vacation even though she went out to cook for a holiday family in the village.

"I hope they get a good price for the house," I said to Alan. "They both work so hard. They deserve a little comfort in their old age." (We actually found out later that both of them were only a couple of years older than us).

Never have I met a gentler, kinder woman than my semi-literate Spanish neighbour. I was very touched when I tried to read the first letter I had from her. There was no punctuation, no capitals and no spaces. Only by reading aloud right across the line could I understand what she was saying. Four pages must have represented hours of effort. I had many friends, French and English, who wouldn't spare half that time.

In order to save the money to pay the bills on the house, I'd been very frugal with myself over these last few years. I had no car of my own, as most of my colleagues had. I'd spent less on clothes which I love and had given up other small luxuries which I'd always taken for granted. I worked hard. Alan seldom put in less than sixty hours a week, but our safe, comfortable, middle-class lives would have been a revelation to our neighbours. I felt a little ashamed of my despondency over a few unplastered walls.

I thought I was prepared for disappointment when we arrived in July. One look at my nearly-new front door showed me that it had been pouring with rain. The lower part was blackened and split by the cascade which must have splashed from the roof. The grey vinyl in the kitchen was still damp where water had seeped underneath, but there was no new ceiling upstairs. For the second time since we'd bought the house, I sat down and wept.

Alan too was very disappointed about the door. "We need a porch," he said, "and the sooner the better."

This meant another job to go on the list. Not for the first time I wondered if we'd bitten off more than we could chew. Perhaps everyone had been right in thinking us crazy to try to get a ruin renovated almost by remote control. I think I even said: "I wanna go home!"

But after a few days in the sunshine, in the wonderful calm and relaxed atmosphere, I recovered from my initial dismay and angry little speeches about broken promises, shutters not done after two years, etc, etc going round in my head. I knew that it was the wrong approach, however, and went off to Laurac with a big smile and summoning all the charm I could.

It was rewarded. Three days later Jean and his brother Roger arrived and spent the whole day putting in new windows and shutters upstairs. Later they fitted a glass porch over the front entrance – another temporary measure that stayed.

With the greatest enthusiasm, we set to work. Alan painted the shutters, whilst I varnished the window frames. This made the downstairs ones look shabby so we did all those again too. As I walked up from the baker's in the morning, we now appeared to have a whole house, even if we still had all the beds downstairs.

There was one interesting but rather alarming feature about our new shutters. In 1965 our bill from the carpenter for three new windows and shutters was 300F. Upstairs there were five windows, all smaller. It had been a difficult job fitting the windows in very irregular openings which had not previously been glazed, but the bill in 1969 was for 1,573F, ie 314F per window instead of 100F.

For the first time we had a larger bill than we anticipated. We just hoped that the estimate given us at Easter for Phase I of the granary conversion would not be increased because of the year's delay.

The porch cost 250F, but was worth every centime as it directed the rainwater well away from the door. The only pity was that we hadn't thought of having it done when the door was new. One evening we had a short, sharp thunderstorm which showed us that it was effective if not terribly aesthetic. Apart from that, during the whole four weeks, we had blazing hot sunshine with one of our visitors going down with a heavy dose of sunstroke.

Although it had been a rather unlucky year in some ways, it was a good year for Jan. She'd done well in her finals and got a good job with Rank Xerox. She'd also been fortunate enough to be left a small legacy by her godmother, Alan's sister Molly, which she received on her 21st birthday. She was driving down in her own car with a student friend, Nick.

It was Nick who got sunstroke, in spite of his dark, Mediterranean skin and our warnings. He was sure he could stand any amount of sun; even the heat on our terrace at mid-day didn't drive him indoors. One morning he got out of bed and fainted. Twenty-four hours on fluids in a darkened room had him back on his feet and no harm done, but since then I've always insisted, against all protests, that no-one stay in the midday sun on the terrace.

Jan and Nick were planning to spend the second part of their holiday in Germany, but were both reluctant to leave. Jan has never acquired the same affection for the country, the food or the language as she has for France. German is very much her second language, whereas Ian loves Spain as much as France, perhaps more, and is equally fluent in both. He was disappointed not to be coming to Ribes this year but had accepted a well paid job at a summer language school through August.

Other people, however, seemed to have decided to come in their hundreds, judging by the number of shoppers in the high street in Joyeuse. The Ardèche was becoming more popular every year. The region is above all wonderful camping country. Campers need food, drink and gas. During July and August the shops worked twelve-hour days, seven days a week and probably made half their yearly profits in these two months.

Incredible though it was, André and Raymonde had finished their house. In six months they'd turned a dismal old place into the most beautiful home – no expense spared, as André didn't lack funds. I've often wondered how different our experience would have been if things hadn't been done on quite such a shoestring.

Our own hopes of completion were miraculously revived when Geo told us that he hoped to complete the new house he was building in the autumn. Better still, a few days later he said that he'd met Jean in Laurac and they'd agreed on a firm date in November to start our work.

For several days Alan and I had been discussing a new idea. We'd always intended to leave the end room downstairs where we still slept as a spare bedroom. Now we thought it would be wasted space. It would be much more sensible to isolate the shower room by building a wall between and extend the living space, with a dining alcove, by pulling down the wall across. We asked Geo to come and have a last talk about all the work and put this to him as well. He could see no problem at all since it was only a partition wall, so it was agreed that this too would be part of the works.

It was vital, of course, that we should have at least one bedroom upstairs at the same time as these downstairs walls were changed. Geo agreed to this, but said that he would plaster the new bedroom only and that the other plastering upstairs would have to be left until Phase II. We didn't like that too much, as we should then be in danger of waiting for him yet again. That's exactly what happened, of course, but at the time we seemed to have no alternative. You take what they offer!

We discussed endlessly plans for the bedrooms. We had dozens, discarded them and resurrected them. We had two unalterable features – the staircase already in place and bathroom plumbing which, for economy, should be in the same position as downstairs. Apart from that, we had approximately 600sq ft to play with. It was rather nice to be able to give ourselves lots of space in the main bedroom having shared with a shower, basin and loo for several years – though we thought we'd probably install a small basin and bidet in the bedroom too eventually.

Our final plan meant we could sleep six people quite easily, and four very comfortably. The proposal for Phase I upstairs was a new tongued-and-grooved pine ceiling, plastering and two fitted wardrobes. Phase II would be the remaining plastering, partitions and bathroom. Both Geo and Jean promised that Phase I would be completed during the winter. We left for England with every hope that when we returned at Easter the following year we shouldn't be disappointed again.

CHAPTER 8

A PROPER BEDROOM

I an left England before we did. Just before Christmas his friend Alan had urgently requested his presence in Brazil, to be best man at his wedding. Ian reluctantly refused as he was committed to his job at the language school until Easter, but he left at the end of March to take up a post in the same organisation as Alan in São Paulo.

Jan had left home in November having found herself a flat share in Baker Street in London. Her office at Xerox was within walking distance, so she was very happy not to have to fight her way to and from work on the Underground every day.

Once again, just before Easter, we were on our own as we loaded the car. We took the grandfather clock with us this time and a few other small bits of furniture, anticipating that we should be able to spread out in the much larger living room.

Although the sun was shining, there was a brisk, cool breeze at Dover.

"I hope it's warmer where we're going."

There wasn't a customs official in sight at Boulogne. We just drove down the ramps and away on to the very familiar switchback road to Paris. We had the heater on all the way and were unprepared for the bitter wind which swirled around us when we stopped at our hotel in Versailles.

In the morning it was snowing hard. As we drove south, the sun came out and rapidly cleared the thin coating of snow on the roads, but on the high plateau beyond Le Puy, the snow ploughs were out, and so were the skiers. Then we ran into thick mist. As we went cautiously round the hairpins, we could see enormous icicles hanging from the rocks. The car heater was still on full as we drove up the ramp into the courtyard.

Through the six days of our stay we never got the temperature to 60°F in the house, but we had lunch three times on the terrace – the sun's always warm.

In spite of the cold, our spirits were high. There were no tears this year. The house looked rather odd inside, but the work was done. With the wall removed, we now had a bed-sitter. The red felt carpet in the sleeping area was almost the same colour as the quarry tiles, but we had some walls beige, some pale green. If you wanted to switch the light on in the alcove, you had to go into the cloakroom.

Upstairs, at last, we had our own bedroom. The ceiling was beautifully done, the wardrobes in, the doors matching the bedroom door. If we'd cared to sleep in caps and mittens and overcoats, with candles only to light us, we could have moved in!

"First call tomorrow, the electrician," I said.

"I'll bet he won't offer to come immediately, like he did the first time," said Alan. We both smiled ruefully because things had changed so much. The Sabouls, their family now increased by twins, like Geo's, had moved from their flat over the shop to a much bigger house. Monsieur Saboul now ran a Peugeot 404; his two assistants and apprentices drove round in large working vans. His wife still looked after the shop, whilst he spent his time going round with a notebook to assess jobs and, rumour had it, stopping for frequent glasses of pastis at any café on his route.

There was a lot to do. We wondered if we had any chance at all of getting the electricity in before the summer. For the moment, it seemed sensible to live and sleep in our one odd room downstairs. At least it would be warmer. We found that, if we left the gas fire on low when we went out in the evening, the room was just bearable to undress in when we got back. Taking a shower in the morning was a decidedly chilly affair – a smart rubdown and many layers of clothing pulled on as quickly as possible. We spent as much time as we could outside, but by 5pm we often had to go for a brisk walk to keep the circulation going!

Our friend, Maurice, had installed oil-fired central heating in his new house, where he'd just spent his first full winter. Oddly enough it had been the coldest winter on record for years. They'd even been snowed up for three days. Very kindly they asked us to move in with them, but, finding that we could manage without too much discomfort, we stayed at La Clède. At the same time we realised that, if ever we wanted to spend a Christmas there – one of my fantasies – we should have to install some better form of heating.

Nor was Maurice's wife very enthusiastic about village life in winter. She remembered evenings in her youth when people gathered in each others' houses in the evenings, the men to play cards, the women to knit and chat and roast chestnuts in the open hearth. Now, after dark, people shuttered themselves in with their television sets. I could imagine that in January, with the daylight gone at 4pm and no street lighting, the village would be like a ghost town. Compared with the animation of the summer – with the shouts and clicks from the various games of *boules* in progress, the laughter of the kids as they played or raced around on their bikes, people strolling around in the cool of the evening, stopping to chat to anyone on their terraces – the lack of communication in the winter would be grim.

Maurice had already decided that he must look for a small flat in Aix en Provence where they could spend December, January and February, coming back to Ribes only when the days were lengthening to start work on their garden.

We couldn't afford to put central heating in La Clède on the chance of an occasional Christmas visit and we were definitely not attracted to the village for a long winter stay. The main object of our life in France was to be outside in the sun. We talked a little about storage heaters before going to see Saboul, but in the end merely asked for more lighting.

He was up very promptly the next day and made notes on what we wanted. The overhead light in the alcove moved into the shower room, three lots of wall lights in the living room, a two-way switch system on the stairs, wall lights and an overhead light in our bedroom with various power points at each location. When he promised to get this done before the summer, we felt so good, we decided to splash out on a new bed and set off to Aubenas after lunch.

Previously, we'd been no more ambitious in our choice of beds than simple divans, but we thought we'd like something a bit more interesting to go with our old beams and furniture. The craze for Victorian brass bedsteads and imitation four posters seemed not to have caught on in France, but we did find a rather nice one. It had head and footboards of slender oak rails, which looked country-style without being too heavy. And, as we'd chosen wall reading lights with oak brackets, it would be in keeping. I say chosen advisedly, since a lot of choice there was not. It was before the days of obsessions with interiors. We'd decided that £100 was our limit and were pleased to pay just a few pounds more for the base and quality mattress – delivery promised for the summer.

Back home, I got out carpet, curtains and bedspread which had last seen the light of day in our old house in Redhill. Plastic bags really are a godsend. There was no sign of moth damage, no speck of dust or fluff.

"I'd forgotten how these looked, but they're OK." I hung up the yellow, mock-patchwork curtains. They exactly touched the floor as if they'd been tailor-made.

"I'll paint the walls a pale yellow, like the kitchen, shall I?" said Alan. "There's still some emulsion left."

"I wish for once I could choose a scheme from scratch," I moaned, "instead of always making do with what we've got."

"It's more of a challenge this way," laughed Alan. "It'll look quite fresh – and the ceiling looks great already." The rough, exposed beams certainly were a lovely old feature against the new pine ceiling.

"Now all we need is the rest of the plastering done, then Jean can finish the other partitions. Laurac tomorrow." We hoped that the 5,000F we were going to pay Jean would put him in a happy and obliging frame of mind. We thanked him for all the beautiful work and asked if he could do the remaining partitions. Again, the same problem – plastering first. Who could do it?

"Suppose we scrape the walls down and leave the bare stone?" I suggested, as we walked back to the car.

"It's a thought, but it would be a hell of a job and bare stone might be a little stark for bedrooms."

Help came from a totally unexpected quarter. When I went to thank Madame Toral for our customary spray of lilies of the valley on our arrival, it was their home in the other part of the house that I visited; they'd sold the bit just across the road from us and so we now had new immediate neighbours.

"Their name is Hernandez," she filled me in. "Yes, of Spanish origin, like us. He was a master builder in Marseille and has retired here because of his health. It's a second marriage on both sides, with married children from the previous marriages. There are two daughters of this marriage, Roberte who's 16 and Nicole, 12."

We soon realised that, ill or no, Monsieur Hernandez was putting in a full day's work every day on his new house. He was repointing the exterior walls in the traditional Ardechois way, scraping out the old mortar and pointing with cement, so that the stones stood out in all their natural beauty. Our walls looked clumsy and amateurish by comparison. When we admired his handiwork, he said "I'm only doing it this way because I've got time to do it myself. To pay someone else to would be expensive. It's tedious work."

As he had just about one third of the wall surface we had, having virtually only half a house, we immediately realised why Geo had not suggested it to us. There had not been the time on his side or the money on ours.

As it was much colder in the house than outside on the terrace, we often chatted to Monsieur Hernandez as he worked away on his ladder. One day, we mentioned our predicament about the plastering and could scarcely believe it when he said he would gladly do it for us when he'd finished his own house. At the same time, he warned us that he had at least a year's work to do but that he would definitely do our plastering before summer 1971.

When we were shown round his house and told of their plans, we fully understood that he had indeed got his work cut out, but we also saw that here was a real craftsman, as opposed to a good workman.

I think perhaps it was at this moment that we realised our troubles were over. We both felt we'd been lucky enough again to meet someone who would not only do what he'd promised, but make an excellent job of it too. We were proved right in this, and also discovered that Roman was one of the kindest, most charming men we had ever met. He had a dry sense of humour which was a delight and appealed to us both, Alan especially, and soon they were enjoying a regular game of boules together. For the next four years part of the joy of La Clède was that we had the Hernandez as neighbours.

Though anxious to accept Roman's offer, I was loath to offend Geo. He and all his family had always been wonderfully kind to us, so I went rather apprehensively to ask him if he minded if Roman did some work for us. No problem; in fact Geo was obviously relieved. He said he was beginning to feel overburdened and unhappy about all the work he was being pressed to do. (Two years later he had a severe breakdown due entirely to strain and overwork). He promised that when work eased off he would still be pleased to do the new terrace at the back of the house to replace the old wooden bridge.

Greatly relieved too, I was then able to confess that not only should we not be retiring in 1971 after all, but that we shouldn't be able to come to France until the summer the next year. Easter 1972 was our new retiring date, and this I intended to hold to whatever the state of the house, though now the prospects were really quite bright. It did at last seem possible that we might finish the work in seven years instead of five as we'd originally – optimistically – planned.

On the day before we left, we struggled upstairs with two single divans, the plastic wardrobe, the chest of drawers and the oak chest. Our old inherited bed, well wrapped in plastic, we stored in the old kitchen in the other half of the house. It had been impossible to get upstairs, so heavy and unwieldy was it. And I confess I hadn't ever had a decent night's sleep in it. It was only 1.20m wide – but cosy in the cold!

At last we were able to arrange our L-shaped living room in a reasonable way. The mahogany, gate-legged 'heirloom' was set up in the alcove with the corner cupboard and grandfather clock. The chairs and the remaining divan were in a much less constricted area now, but we had a new problem, of course.

Since the wall had been removed, there was a slight but obvious difference in floor levels. The main room was quarry tiled; the alcove cement (covered in the red felt). Should we raise the level in the alcove even more and make a dining platform covered with matching quarry tiles? Should we discard the existing quarry tiles and have a completely new wooden floor? Roman had done this in one of his rooms. Perhaps a combination of rush matting and tiles? But for the moment, the extra bedrooms were the priority.

We went to Lablachère for dinner. Janet was expecting a baby, whom we should meet on our next trip. They too were soon to embark on a complete modernisation of the hotel.

As we went back into our house I looked with my usual disgust at the grey vinyl on the kitchen floor which was all chipped and broken now in the doorway. Before we'd put up the temporary porch, the rainwater had come in and soaked it so often it had begun to disintegrate. We'd always dreamed that one day we'd be able to have a tiled floor. Now, wise after the event, we realised that we should have done this right at the beginning when it would have been infinitely cheaper. Today's prices made it out of the question. I realised I was going to have to live with Marley tiles – *c'est la vie*. It's certainly been my life!

The kitchen as a whole needed a face-lift anyway. I wanted more worktop and storage, but this was at the bottom of the priorities list at the moment. I'd paid Geo 1,320F for his share of the work already done. I should owe the electrician in the summer. We ourselves had our own list of DIY jobs: paint the bedroom walls, stain all the doors and floors, line the wardrobes ...

I was beginning to be very conscious of the fact that after December 1971 there would be no more money coming into my bank account. I still felt annoyed about the year when almost nothing had been done. It was to be a race against time and a fight to pay the bills, which were now always a little more than we'd anticipated and certainly more than the year before. Unfortunately for us, whatever was happening in the world economic situation, we always seemed to lose ground and get a poorer exchange against the franc.

In this mood, I usually got out my file, checked over the bills and made forward estimates. In April 1970, ie five years after paying our first bill, the grand total for all work done was 25,592F. We'd also paid 2,295F for vinyl, a cooker, plastic wardrobe, fridge and bed. After averaging out the fluctuating rate of exchange I arrived at a figure of around £2,250.

In return for this we had a good terrace, a pleasant, functional kitchen, a comfortable living room, a shower room and loo and a lovely big bedroom. Rates, gas and electricity cost us very little more than £25pa. Five weeks holiday a year over the past five years would have cost us far more than this had they been spent in hotels. I immediately felt better.

I was quite anxious to get back home for once. We were looking forward to Ian's first letter from Brazil and anticipating that he'd want a lot of things sent out to him. All seemed to be well. At first he'd stayed with friend Alan and his new wife, Lala. She was of Polish origin, her parents having only been in São Paulo since the end of World War II. These young friends smoothed his path considerably in the first few weeks, so we were pleased to send some things for Alan as well. The most daunting thing on Ian's list was all his albums.

"We can't possibly send them all," I said to (husband) Alan. "He must have at least 300. Choose 100 for him."

The letters from Brazil continued to be interesting and entertaining – both our children write good letters – with descriptions of life in SP, Rio, weekends at country houses and the highly demanding work at the Cultura with its 8,000 students. Ian was looking forward to the long Christmas holiday when he could really explore the country a little. He was talking about either going up the Amazon by canoe, or pony-trekking in Argentina!

What he actually did in the end was quite different. He rang us up on Christmas Eve to tell us he was getting married to a girl called Eliane and they would be going on their honeymoon in January. Eliane was Brazilian, also on the staff at the Cultura. When we'd recovered from the shock, we wrote asking for a photo and more details. These duly arrived – we had a dish of a daughter-in-law!

When we went back to the cottage at the end of July, Jan came with us, promising to tackle the garden whilst we did the bedroom. We were all a little dismayed when we drove up the ramp. The whole courtyard was a sea of weeds. In the flowerbeds she'd made, the pinks, roses, mimosa even, all overrun – there were weeds everywhere.

The shutters and door were wide open. True to form, the electricians were working, alerted by dear Roman to the date of our arrival. The downstairs lighting was finished; the rest would be done the next day.

On 1 August Alan and I slept upstairs in a real bedroom on our new bed which had been delivered that morning. We made Jan comfortable in the rather large remaining space. The next morning we all got to work. Jan started weeding, in her bikini, as always. I started on the varnishing; Alan began the walls.

The main bedroom is a very spacious and pleasant room, and furnished and painted, it looked great. The small piece of carpet we'd allocated was not large enough, which meant I was down on my knees again, scraping plaster off the floor – not terribly successfully – prior to staining and varnishing the bits that showed! I'd bought us something new for it this year. Instead of the usual making-do with cast-offs or stuff from the Green Shield stamp catalogue – some yellow cotton bedlinen. We lay in bed that night and laughed like kids at the pleasure of it all.

"Something's got to go wrong," said Alan. "The rail in the wardrobe will snap any minute." But this time, no disasters.

Jan had tidied up beautifully outside. All our geranium pots were in place, the terrace and garden neat once more. We had yellow roses in the living room and a beautiful display of branches and wild flowers in the kitchen hearth.

The completion of Phase I marked the beginning of the transformation of La Clède from a holiday house, where standards of comfort were not to be taken too seriously, into a home. Though I often still got impatient with dilatory workmen and other hassles, I never again despaired.

"Right, that's enough work for this year," I said. "Let's enjoy ourselves now!"

We swam. We went to the jazz club. We visited the local sights – Vallon Pont d'Arc, Thines, Notre Dame des Neiges, behaving like tourists for the first time rather than residents. Nowadays, it's possible to book all kinds of arranged holidays, but in 1970 most of the visitors were campers or people like our friends who had summer homes in the area. It was very busy in August. Sometimes over a hundred young people tried to squeeze into the club on a Saturday night and it really did get too close for comfort.

Jan had to leave in mid-August. It was a horrible shock for her, after having student vacations, to be tied down to just a couple of weeks holiday. (She's never got over it! Ed). We thought we'd be on our own for the second part of our holiday, but we had two unexpected sets of visitors. First, some ex-neighbours who stayed five days and then a young colleague of Alan's, John Disley, with his wife and two young children.

"I thought it was time I fulfilled an ambition," said John. "I want to canoe down the Ardèche." Alan asked if he meant to take a few days, camping on the way.

"Good heavens, no," said John. "I should be able to do it in about six hours."

"And I'm going to drive along the road and pick him up at the far end," said wife Sylvia. Even for John, who was an international athlete, this seemed a little ambitious.

By good fortune, on the day set for the trip, it was comparatively cool. At 11am John put his canoe in the water at Pont d'Arc. At 5pm Sylvia parked the car downstream at St Enémie just as John pulled his canoe up onto the beach. She'd not seen him once *en route* in spite of numerous stops but had been very thrilled with the drive. John said it was one of the most beautiful trips he'd ever made, the canoeing not too difficult and the scenery incredible. He added that he'd seen some beautiful girls too who'd done nothing but embellish the scenery! We knew there were several nudist camps in the gorges and were in total agreement that the conditions were ideal to dispense with clothes altogether to enjoy the sun and water. They said they couldn't wait to come again when the girls were a little older and do the trip as a family.

During their stay there was one small snag. Our dining table was inadequate for six. I'd always intended to ask the carpenter to make me a table but realised it would take forever to commission one. We decided to go hunting in the antique shops in Alès and Uzès. It was a wasted journey – the prices were sky-high; the tables often completely worm-ridden.

On the way home from this long, hot trip we stopped for a drink in a little town just before Janet's hotel. In the window of an odd, little shop in a back street, standing rather forlornly by itself was exactly what we were looking for – a simple, refectory table, handmade in solid chestnut. It was delivered the next day and was perfect for the alcove.

"Chairs, next year," I smiled at Alan. "We need four more." These were added to the shopping list. I hoped we'd have enough money. For the first time we left the key with dear Roman, confident that when we returned the following July, the plastering would have been done.

CHAPTER 9

LOSE A FLOOR – GAIN A DOOR

In 1971 we reached another small milestone in our lives. We celebrated our 30th wedding anniversary. We'd always hoped to begin our retirement at Easter of this year and spend our first full summer at La Clède. Instead, in late March we went on an educational cruise with 1,200 students, 80 teachers and 200 private passengers. We visited Venice and Naples, Athens, Crete and Tunis. We'd love to return to Greece and Italy one day.

In Crete we bought the doorbell for La Clède at a very superior gift shop in the main square of Heraklion. It was the soft blue that caught my eye – some of the stone in the house is the same colour – and on closer inspection I saw the grapevine design and thought it would suit. The prices of the alabaster figures and onyx ashtrays that others were buying were staggering; the bell was reasonable.

We put it up when we arrived at the end of July in a heatwave. Jan and new friend Bruce were already there. For the first time the weeds were cleared; all was tidy in the house and even the plastering was done! I asked Madame Hernandez if she'd mind if I gave her husband a big hug. He got a smacking kiss on both cheeks too, so delighted was I to see no further obstacles to the final stage of our conversion.

Alan and Roman were by now good friends and got on wonderfully well together in spite of occasional problems of communication. A most interesting development this year was the growing friendship/romance between Roberte, their beautiful elder daughter, and Christian, the eldest of Geo's sons. They were soon to be separated, as Roberte was going to Marseille to train as a nurse and Christian to Orange to do his military service. Perhaps because of this, though they were both very young, the parents had agreed to an engagement.

"It can't last surely," I said pessimistically to Alan. "Imagine Roberte surrounded by all those young medical students and doctors."

"Christian's a bit of a looker too," Alan added. "I'm sure he won't lack for female company either, if he wants it."

Little Ghiselaine, Christian's sister, who'd been happy to sit on Alan's knee a few years ago, was now as tall as me. She was nearly 12, the age of confirmation, and had grown into a very attractive young girl.

On the day of the engagement party we kept indoors as far as possible. Our terraces are very close to each other and we assumed it would be a family affair and wanted to keep out of their way. At 6pm Roberte rang the bell and said everyone was waiting for us. I never failed to be touched by this assumption that we would be included in any of their festivities. (It continues to this day. Ed)

I was amazed when I saw the food spread, not so much at its variety and quantity – Madame Hernandez is an excellent cook – as at its sophistication. There was smoked salmon, caviar, cheese *choux*, stuffed eggs, giant prawns, anchovy toasts and many other savouries which wouldn't have disgraced an embassy reception. I thought of the wonderful but homely meals we'd shared in the past with the Torals and the Balazucs and could only be a little sad at what family entertaining had become. I confess though that this was only a passing thought and that I munched away with relish, as did all the relatives, the eight or nine young children and the couple's young friends! There was a magnificent *pièce montée* to finish – with champagne, of course – a great pyramid of cream-filled *choux* coated with coffee icing and caramel.

Afterwards the men went off to play boules, delighted for once to have two good teams – *Ribois vs Etrangers*. Alan was asked to play for the Ribois – he was tickled pink. The children went off to amuse themselves; the women cleared up and settled down for a good gossip on the terrace. We could hear the exclamations, joking and mild cursing that always accompany a match. These continued until it was so dark we could hardly distinguish the figures in the road.

Alan told me later that, rather than abandon the game, they'd continued with two of the kids shining torches on the *bouchon* or jack. They'd been playing for over two hours and the most reluctant to stop was a Balazuc uncle aged 87! The *Ribois* won.

With the men back with raging thirsts, there was more wine brought out, the local red this time. Then, finally, the country tradition of huge bowls of home-made soup with fresh bread, followed by goat's cheese and the most wonderful sweet melons. A final glass of champagne was served to drink the young couple's health. At nearly midnight we climbed the steps to our terrace feeling more than a little lightheaded. Thank goodness we didn't have far to go!

Three nights later we came home at the same time in the same state! A first Communion really is a family affair. Thirty-two members of the Balazuc family had sat down to lunch on their enormous terrace. Ghiselaine had been to see us in the morning to show off her white dress and veil. She brought us the usual invitation.

"Gran says please come over this evening."

We thought it would be just for a drink, so we finished our garden watering and strolled along the road in working gear (shorts/shirts). We were desperately embarrassed to find twenty-two elegantly dressed people sitting at the table waiting for us.

"I'm so sorry, Madame," I said, trying to look as unobtrusive as possible as I slipped into a vacant seat next to Geo, who, lovely man he is, squeezed my hand and pecked my cheek in welcome.

"We had no idea. We're thrilled to be with you all." I smiled, somewhat overcome, around the whole circle. We were so touched, yet again, to be accepted with such warmth into this family gathering.

The meal was a far more sophisticated version of our well-remembered Balazuc feasts. We had prawns, creamed mushrooms, cold meats and salads and an enormous icecream *gâteau* to finish. It lasted four hours and was utterly delightful from start to finish.

We gave our anniversary party in our favourite mountain inn at Sanilhac. All our friends from Joyeuse, Paris, Nimes and Brittany were with us. At the end of the meal they presented us with six cut-glass whisky tumblers. With tears in my eyes, I thanked them all for their company and friendship – for taking us in, in fact. Both with them and with our village friends and neighbours we felt entirely at home and accepted and could only look forward eagerly to the long summers of retirement to come.

With all this party going and giving we did very little work at the house. There was, in fact, little we could do except water and keep the weeds down. We'd made rough beds all round the courtyard and must have moved dozens of buckets of stones, remnants of the old silkhouse, in the process.

We were delighted because the lilac had revived itself. It had bloomed in the spring, Madame Hernandez told us, after the mimosa. The virginia creeper was very healthy and growing fast, but it needed something to climb over. Time for a frame to be made.

We went back to our handsome plumber. For him, as for the electrician, things had changed a lot since we'd first asked for his help.

"He's got half a dozen men working for him now," said Geo, "and he has work as far away as Montpellier. Wait till you see his new house. Unfortunately, it all seems to have gone to his head."

"What do you mean?" I asked.

"Well, he seems to need more than one wife. He's always taking women off for the weekend."

"I can't say I'm that surprised. I shouldn't think he has to ask twice. He's extremely handsome, after all."

Geo laughed and looked a little disapproving, but I could see Jeanine agreed with me.

Claude's new house was just on the outskirts of Joyeuse – not a house really, a very large flat over a huge workshop and garages. When he answered our ring at the door, he shook us by the hand and smiled, "Mr and Mrs Anderson, how are you? Come in and have a drink." An exact repeat of the first time at Roger's bar.

This time, though, two things were very evident. He most certainly wouldn't be putting in our new bathroom himself, nor would the bill be as modest as before.

He drove up the next day in a Citroën DS and wrote down careful notes of our requirements. We needed another loo, a basin and a bath. I wanted to leave some space for possible storage or a bidet one day, so we plumped for a small Dutch bath with a seat. Everything in white and we'd do the tiling ourselves.

"You'll need a much larger water heater," said Claude. "I'll take the other back in part exchange."

We also explained about the car port and the frame for the terrace. "All quite simple," he said. "When would you like all this done?"

I told him that Jean, the carpenter, would be coming in the autumn to do the partition walls and that I'd ask him to ring up when he'd finished. "It will be done, Madame."

"After that lot, we'll need Saboul again to do the electrics and that'll be it," I said to myself. "At least for the moment." I always made this silent reservation because one day I intended to do the old wing too.

The estimate, which arrived two days later, was not quite as bad as we'd feared: 3,240F. I got out my file to find the old bills for the shower room and the loo.

Altogether, including the kitchen sink and water heater, we'd already paid the plumber £200. It was not the plumber's fault that in 1972, because of the poor exchange rate, we had to find £300 to pay his bill.

"It's almost unbelievable that we've had all the plumbing done for £500," Alan said. "Of course, it's partly because of easier regulations."

We'd already discussed the placing of the bedroom and bathroom partition walls with Jean. Now that we'd seen the plumber, we could draw everything out on the floor. We bought some chalks and spent an agreeable hour drawing, loo and all.

To our surprise, Geo was suddenly free to replace the broken-down wooden bridge which led from the granary to the back garden. I asked him also, whilst doing that, if he could build up the retaining wall too.

"That means we need new doors for the granary," Alan said. "We might as well have them in the same style as the front." So, it would be light oak and glass panels again.

Sitting in the lounge at the end of a rare cloudy day, Alan said, "You know, this room would look better and be lighter if we had a glass-panelled door into the kitchen. And a plain one into the shower room. I groaned inwardly – more expense, my ceramic tile kitchen floor finally gave up the ghost.

"You're right, it would. But if we have new doors here, it's definitely Marley tiles in the kitchen and shower."

"Do you mind very much? Perhaps the doors are more important. It's as black as Hades in here when the sun doesn't shine."

Next day I asked Roman where to get Marley tiles. He suggested a firm in Aubenas. Compared with the range of colour and design we were used to in England, there was very little choice indeed, the least offensive thing being a pale yellowy beige, slightly marbled with white.

Within two days we were walking on our new kitchen floor. The old grey vinyl was burnt in the courtyard and we were planning the colour schemes for the face lift.

Carpets are not commonly seen in the south of France. Our friends had chosen various ceramic floor styles for their elegant lounges. My red quarry tiles were right for the house's style, which after all was only a modest country house. But the wear and tear on my knees applying Cardinal Red had already been considerable. And there's no easier cleaning than hoovering. Contrary to local custom, therefore, and at the risk of being 'bourgeois' (!), we decided to cover the whole floor, alcove included, with the same cord carpet. The old pale green Wilton could then be used in the 'spare room', the blue rugs in the guest room and the red felt in the corridor.

Once this was decided, the colour schemes began to shape themselves. During the last few days of our stay, we spent hours measuring and calculating paint and wallpaper quantities, and new carpet for the lounge. The list of items to bring the following year grew and grew. For a stay of four months, we'd need things we'd managed without until now, like an ironing board and iron, a Hoover, a food mixer, more gardening tools, a radio, stereo, more clothes ... We'd already planned to buy a new car when we retired. Perhaps it would have to be another stationwagon!

The day before leaving we worked all day in our 'garden'. There'd been a heavy storm in the night which had left the earth manageable for once. Normally, it bakes hard in the summer sun. We cleared hundreds more stones and tidied up the rough beds round the edges of the courtyard. Roman came to visit and said he might have time to tackle one of the back terraces during the winter. If he cleared the top one, he'd plant potatoes. He'd be pleased to have use of more land nearer his house for watering purposes, since his *potager* (vegetable garden) was about a mile away with no source, which made it useless in summer.

This watering ritual was one of the biggest headaches in the south of France. A lawn was out of the question – even flowers and vegetables were not easy to grow without a lot of watering, but we were determined to have a try when we were more established. We also wanted to get rid of our old fruit trees and plant some new ones – peaches and cherries. At least in April and May we'd be able to work outside without wilting in the heat.

The last day came. We went round to say our goodbyes with a light heart, knowing that we only had a few more months to work.

Back in England, it was a very hectic last term for both of us – exhausting, exhilarating, often amusing, but a little sad too. We were thoroughly spoiled – wined and dined, presented with lovely gifts and warmed by many kind words.

The usual Christmas celebrations followed. Ian was still in Brazil. His last letter in January was full of plans for a long trip around South America that he intended to make with Eliane. Bruce and Jan spent Christmas day with us. We knew that Bruce was pressing her to name a wedding date, but she seemed unsure. We both begged her to be careful not to make a mistake. However, at the end of February, they were married. Jan moved into Bruce's flat in London and we wished them well.

In March we began to turn our thoughts back to paints and wallpaper. I've always been fascinated by home decor magazines, but the homes they feature are often so glamourised that they're simply frustrating. Surely most people are like us and have to do their own decorating, run up their own curtains and work to a strict budget. It would be a delightful change for us to plan a room from start to finish without having to fit in existing items. Ingenuity has always had to make up for lack of cash. Our blue guest room at La Clède is a good example of this.

We started off with hand-made (1941) blue wool rugs, lined blue check gingham curtains inherited in some house, and two single beds – cast offs of my sister's – which we'd brought from Geneva on our roof rack. We had an attractive half-moon table to act as a dressing table. For the walls, we were lucky to find a Mary Quant wallpaper called Gingham. Two rolls were enough for the wall behind the beds. The other walls were to be plain white emulsion with pictures.

I bought 12 yards of a cotton dress fabric at 39p a yard, a small floral print of pale and dark blue flowers on a white background, which I made into two throwover covers. To finish off, I found two royal blue frilled pillowcases to go over like cushions. It cost very little but looked pretty good when I spread all the samples out in England.

We were very anxious to avoid a chintzy, olde worlde effect in the sitting room. Fortunately, the ceilings are high – no danger of headbanging on the beams – and it's roomy. The furniture is country antique. There was no way we could strive for elegance.

We chose the carpet first – plain old gold – and finally settled on a paper and matching Liberty print in a small yellow flower design on white. The window walls would be plain white. We felt the full-length curtains (same pattern) would be good against this.

Schemes for kitchen and bathroom remained. After doing five kitchens up until then, my favourite, freshest-looking was blue and white. At La Clède we already had some blue and white tiles as part of the old cooker built into the wall next to the fireplace. I'd always wanted to follow that through, but had always been more dependant on the colour of things I already had. It happened again this time. We needed more storage and more worktop. We went shopping. The only suitable thing we could find was olive green Formica, currently all the rage in France, but not at all what we really wanted. So, once again, need overrode aesthetics – we would have an olive green kitchen! We found an attractive paper, so all was well if not perfect.

We'd had a Christmas card from Jean telling us that he'd finished the partition work and notified the plumber. Our second bathroom was being done! One of the things we'd come to dislike thoroughly was pastel bathroom suites, especially pink, a particular favourite in France. At La Clède all the sanitaryware was white and we wanted the minimum of tiles, finding the all-tile look somewhat cold and clinical. We found a paper – the most expensive of the batch – in browns and oranges, a very '60s paisley design, which we thought with dark brown tiles and beige floor would be light and warm (I'd never forgotten the temperature that Easter). I treated us and it to new matching bath towels and bathmat. With 20 books of Green Shield stamps I got a bathroom cabinet and an Ali Baba linen basket.

As all these purchases began to accumulate in the spare room in Weybridge, we began to wonder if our new Renault 16 was going to be big enough. I'd already collected everything on the list but forgotten books.

Wherever we've lived in England we've taken it for granted that we had easy access to a public library. In France these are limited to a few large towns. All my life I've read up to six books a week and simply couldn't imagine a life with nothing to read. I'd been collecting paperbacks and second-hand books in batches for years. Many were already in France, but this year we wanted to take two bookcases together with reading books, files, dictionaries and other reference books, not to mention my cookery books.

The real spanner in the works was the carpet. The company began to make so many difficulties and excuses about delivering it to France, having said it was no problem before the sale, that in the end Alan lost patience and said we'd take it ourselves. When it arrived and was dumped on the hall floor, it looked like two Grecian temple columns.

Alan bought a heavy duty roof rack. He assured me the carpet was no heavier than the two beds we'd taken already, but I was apprehensive. We made final lists of people to see, letters to write, addresses to note, things to take; insurance was arranged, tickets booked, currency and travellers cheques obtained, mail redirected ... We really could think of nothing left to do.

At 11am on take-off day, there wasn't a square inch of space in the car and my sewing machine was still in the drive. Everything else was in which was little short of miraculous. We were amazed and pleased. We thought we'd have to pay some customs duty this time as the carpet was new, but hoped they wouldn't be too strict.

We had a picnic lunch, left a welcome home card on the table for Ian and Eliane, expected home from Brazil in July, and drove very slowly out of the road with all the neighbours waving us off. Retirement starts here! We had to catch the 4.30pm ferry at Dover and didn't intend to drive very far that evening in France.

We scarcely spoke on the way down. I think we were both exhausted and I couldn't relax until we were through French customs. It was a beautiful afternoon, a calm sea, an almost empty boat. We were the only car to drive into the red zone at customs. The officials were extremely courteous and charged us a small sum for the carpet import.

We began to relax as we drove along the road to Montreuil in the evening sun, but there was one more anxiety. We'd planned to stay in the motel just outside Abbeville, but it was closed. In all the preparations I'd forgotten that we'd be travelling out of season. We wanted security overnight for our precious cargo, but couldn't find a hotel with any garage or yard. I spent a somewhat restless night, wondering if all would still be there in the morning.

I needn't have worried. It also didn't rain during the journey. We rolled along very smoothly, barely aware of the load, but thankful all the same as we drove carefully down the Ardèche valley on the last lap.

Our spirits were high. We'd never been in our corner of France at this time of year before. The sun shone on a countryside more beautiful than we'd ever seen it.

CHAPTER 10

FINAL TOUCHES

We drove through a fairytale world. Flowers which at home follow each other in sedate sequence were growing here simultaneously in mad profusion. The slopes of the mountains were golden with broom and gorse. The lower meadows were a patchwork of fresh, green grass, white narcissi and blue scyllas. Along the same stretch of road we saw cowslips and wild roses. When we drove up the ramp into our courtyard, the lilac and roses were in bloom together.

All the doors and windows in the house were wide open as usual. We went in and straight upstairs as we could hear voices. True to form, Geo and his brother, Serge, were still working on the new back terrace. Pipes trailed from the taps in the new bathroom basin across the floor, and one was leaking. Everything was filthy, covered with plaster and cement dust, all well trodden in and soaked. The new external oak doors were splashed with cement. The floor of the middle guest room was inches deep in sawdust and shavings. Downstairs in the living room the furniture was thankfully covered with dust-sheets, as we usually left it in the winter. The new internal oak doors were beautiful.

We heard voices outside on the front terrace – Nicole and Ghiselaine, both prettier than ever, had arrived to help.

"Where shall we put these?" they kept asking as they arrived at the front door with endless boxes and bags from the car.

"Just leave everything here in the kitchen for the moment, thank you, my darlings," I replied, thankful that I had one clean surface at least. The carpet, the paint and wallpaper, the garden tools we put in the old kitchen next door, but when everything else had been unloaded, it was scarcely possible to move our feet between the suitcases and boxes on our new kitchen floor.

"Thank you again, girls," we said. "See you tomorrow when we're sorted out a bit more."

It was lunch time and Geo and Serge soon followed them home. We stood and looked at the chaos we now had to organise.

"I've a dreadful headache," I confessed to Alan.

"So have I," he replied. "Let's make a cuppa, take some codeine and sit for five minutes."

After drinking our tea in complete silence, we suddenly looked at each other and realised that in spite of all the mess and confusion, this was the end. This was the dream come true. We were here and it didn't really matter when we did anything!

"Alan, we did it, didn't we? They all thought we were mad, but we've done it." And I jumped up and hugged him. It was a moment of supreme satisfaction and contentment.

Nevertheless, on that first afternoon it didn't seem possible that we could get things straight even in the four months of our stay. We had invited two of our oldest friends to visit us in June and had in fact only six weeks to make the house fit for guests.

Geo and Serge finished the terrace on Saturday, the day after we arrived. They had rebuilt two feet of the retaining wall. I hoped they'd be back on Monday to finish it but wasn't really surprised when they didn't show up.

We had too much to do ourselves to worry about it. All day Saturday we were unpacking and sorting. At least we had our own bedroom which was clean and tidy. We kept the door firmly closed and had a small fan heater to keep us moderately warm. Without this one room as a haven of normality, I think we should have become very depressed during the next week or two, because at first it seemed impossible to keep the house clean and warm.

We moved the gas fire and two comfortable chairs into the kitchen whilst Alan tackled the living room. On Roman's advice, we'd given up the idea of sanding the beams – it would have made so much dust – so the first job was to paint them and dark brown seemed the obvious choice. Meanwhile, I set about cleaning upstairs. When I'd swept it all, I realised I'd have to scrape the new floor inch by inch and reseal it.

By Sunday evening we were both exhausted. Alan took a shower but I decided to try my new bath. I turned on the tap, closed the shutters and automatically put out a hand to switch on the light. Nothing there, of course, but the first bath by candlelight was wonderful.

"No work tomorrow," I said as I started to make the evening meal. "We must go to see Saboul, so we might as well go to Laurac to see Jean and to Aubenas to choose some dining chairs."

We were greeted with big smiles and handshakes at Laurac, but we couldn't get a commitment to do any work. They were snowed under. We went into the office to pay our bill and were joined by Jean's wife for the usual drink. Geo had told us that they were having a new house built, so I asked her how they were getting on.

"Oh, it's nearly finished," she said. "The central heating's in and all the bathroom and kitchen equipment."

"What's holding you up then?"

"Well, I haven't a single shelf or cupboard yet," she said. "What I need is a carpenter!"

We all laughed. "Other people's business always comes first, doesn't it?" We left realising that now all our major carpentry work was done, we'd never get the Tourel brothers back to do our small odds and sods. "I'll have a go myself," said Alan valiantly.

We found some high-backed, rush-seat chairs which would go with our dining table and asked for them to be delivered the following weekend. Next we went back to the place we'd bought the Marley tiles for some flooring for the new bathroom. Back in Joyeuse, Saboul's wife promised that she'd ask him to come up to the village as soon as possible. Lastly, a visit to the supermarket to stock up on food and then all missions were accomplished. For the rest of the week we didn't leave the village except to have a meal out at Janet's hotel.

While Alan painted beams, painted and papered the living room walls, I made up the curtains, paper-lined the wardrobe shelves, worked on the floors upstairs and generally acted as decorator's mate whenever necessary, as well as being chief cook and bottle washer.

Each morning and afternoon we looked out hopefully for Saboul's DS. By Saturday, we'd decided another call was necessary. Then the postman arrived with a tale which dashed our hopes completely.

The postman in a country area is, of course, the district grapevine. He's the only person who regularly calls at some of the more remote farms, so he knows what's going on everywhere. He brings all the local news, births, deaths, engagements, weddings, houses for sale, accidents or any sudden illnesses. This Saturday there was a different headline.

"You know about the robberies?"

"Robberies?!" (Unheard of in those days). "No, where?"

"In Joyeuse. Three shops have been broken into and ransacked. They must have had a big van. Saboul's got nothing left."

We pictured his shop in the high street, with no room to move between the piles of electrical appliances.

"Poor Saboul," we said. "Let's hope he was well insured and knows what he had in stock. Tell him we're so sorry."

Sympathetic we were, but also down at heart on our own account. We resigned ourselves to the fact that we wouldn't be seeing him for a while. When he eventually walked up to the terrace ten days later, our usually cheerful electrician looked so ill. We put a whisky in his hand and listened to his tale of woe.

"I lost at least 50,000F worth of stock," he said. "Maybe more. I couldn't remember everything I had. It'll take months to replace." We commiserated. He sighed, downed his drink and said, "Might as well get started."

After he'd made notes on our requirements upstairs, we asked him, for about the tenth time, to let us pay what we owed him so far, for work he'd done two years before.

"Oh, don't worry about that now. Pay me it all when the work's finished." He promised to send two men up the following week.

We had a real tough job to do the next day. As the living room decorating was finished, it was carpet-laying time – another first. It was 6ft wide and incredibly awkward to manoeuvre. It took us the whole of a backbreaking, exhausting day.

I remembered the man who'd done the kitchen floor. He'd had all the same problems – walls not straight, corners not true – but he'd finished at lunch time. The young man who'd put down the flooring in the new bathroom took just over an hour in spite of all the awkward bits round the loo and basin. We were both on our hands and knees until 5pm. What amateurs, what swearing! It's the sort of thing that's truly hell at the time, but you laugh like a drain about it afterwards.

We had a brief rest and a cuppa, then started to move the furniture back in. Then we put up the curtains and a few pictures, appraising the effect. We decided in the end that we'd erred, if anything, on the conservative side, but that the general feel was light and fresh as we'd wanted. The carpet was a reasonable success – it unified the room at least. The only remaining eyesore was the stairway. The new and huge upright pillar at its base was still bare wood, but pointless to treat it until we had some kind of handrail fitted and the whole thing looked more finished. I could see by the look in Alan's eyes that he was already considering how to tackle it.

I cut some yellow roses and put them on the table in an old silver teapot, then set the table with a new tablecloth and candles for our first dinner in the finished room. One of our favourite records of all time, and our hymn of joy, is Duke Ellington's Satin Doll. Live, the music's wild and there's a deluge of applause at the end. We played it after dinner.

The next day Alan was deep in consultation with Roman about the staircase. By evening it had four slim vertical safety rails and the corners of the monster upright had been softened with strips of beading. The staining and polishing could begin. My job and one I tackled with enthusiasm.

What we'd have done without the help and unfailing kindness of our neighbour I do not know. Whenever they went out he brought across the key to his cellar workshop, in case Alan wanted to use any of his tools. We were already very much in his debt for all the work he'd put in in the garden through the winter.

The retaining terrace wall of the top level of land below the road had always been smothered in old vines and brambles. We'd been astonished when we arrived to see a beautiful 6ft high stone wall in almost perfect condition. I was quite sure that Roman had rebuilt some of it, but he said not. He'd found it like that when he'd hacked away all the old growth. He'd cleared the land of weeds and gone over it again and again with a rotocultivator. A wonderful crop of potatoes was almost ready to dig up for us all to share.

In the rough flower beds in the courtyard he'd planted some beans, tomatoes and strawberries. Madame Hernandez had put in some petunias and yellow dahlias. With lots of watering, everything was thriving, despite the poor soil.

Inside, the kitchen was next on the Job Sheet. It is always unpleasant when the heart of the home is in chaos and food has to be prepared amongst paint, paste and paper. Fortunately we could eat picnic lunches outside. The sun was strong now and the house was starting to warm up a bit, though it was still cool in the evenings. Alan pressed on in the same sequence – beams, wallpapering and painting, cupboards, now olive green to match our new unit. It slowly began to grow on us, but then it had to! But I've never really liked it; hardly any of it was really what I wanted. Compromise all along the line.

As each day saw the kitchen nearer completion, I began to fret again about the upstairs electricity. We couldn't do much work up there without the wiring being done first. Whenever we went to Joyeuse, we smiled big smiles into Saboul's shop and made enquiring looks, but by the Saturday we finished the kitchen, no-one had yet shown up.

But downstairs was finished. Appropriately enough the next day was Whit Sunday, so we decided to have a day off. The Hernandez were entertaining Maurice and Georgette, his wife, to lunch. As we sat eating our modest little working lunch outside, Nicole came across with some home-made strawberry tarts. Roman followed soon after with a bottle of champagne in his hand. We begged them to join us so that we could all enjoy it together. It was a near perfect day – vivid blue sky, no wind, with the sun not yet hot enough to make you seek shade. Alan was smiling broadly as we raised our glasses. "Peg, I'm a truly happy man," he said. "And what truly wonderful neighbours."

"Try it in French, my love, go on." He did slowly, heavily encouraged by all. They seemed totally delighted at his efforts, and I remember it as one of our happiest moments.

At 3pm we all set off for a walk in the woods. Georgette had spent all her summer holidays in the village as a child and knew every path. She led us for miles up through the forest on tracks we'd never explored ourselves. We came across houses romantically tucked away in little clearings or on the edge of some ravine in complete isolation.

When we got back the men went off to play *boules*, while the women inspected the work to date and were kindly complimentary about it all. There's no doubt that downstairs was a transformation and very different from the local style. It was a wonderful day and we yet again counted our blessings for being where we were instead of at home, preparing for the last, always hectic weeks of the summer term. But it was back to work the following day.

We spent it varnishing and polishing all the new doors upstairs and the new oak doors onto the back terrace. It was a most pleasant working temperature now; no need for sweaters and not yet the crushing heavy heat of July and August.

Next morning, when it was finally obvious that no electricians were on their way, we went down to Joyeuse to make our last plea. We now had only ten days before our guests arrived. We got a definite promise from Madame Saboul that someone would come the next day,

But we knew her power on the work front was limited. By Wednesday, still no-one and we were seething with frustration. This was something we couldn't do ourselves – Alan drew the line at electrics and plumbing – and something not even Roman could help with. We were sitting on the terrace after lunch wondering what to do about it all when a large van began slowly to reverse up the ramp. This was cause for amazement in itself, since it's no easy matter to negotiate forwards. When they finally came to rest, we both cheered.

I didn't feel like cheering two hours later when I saw my bedroom. They'd been hacking at the wall in order to get the wires though to the meter below and my polished floor was inches deep in plaster. Soon the whole top floor was once more covered in dust. They cheerfully told me that I should have had all the wiring done before the plastering. I managed to hold my tongue for once, but inside I swore at all French workmen.

There was absolutely no point trying to clean up until they'd finished which they'd said would be Saturday. Over optimistic indeed. They didn't even show up on Saturday and it wasn't until Monday lunchtime that the job was completed. We were hopping mad; it left us just five days to complete the decorating before the arrival of our guests on Saturday.

Fortunately we didn't need to do anything to the beams upstairs. It was just a question of walls and floors. Once again I was on my hands and knees trying to repair the damage, while Alan worked all day with brushes and rollers, paint and paper. By Thursday, he'd started the bathroom. We also had to go shopping to stock up with food and I had to cook, so it was nearly midnight on Friday before we both fell into bed exhausted.

The next day we had a quick clean up all through the house. When our friends, Ruth and Joan arrived at 6pm, we were sitting on the terrace with a drink, looking completely at home and relaxed, but actually aching in virtually every joint, knees bruised and blistered, hands work-worn and Alan with slight double vision from cracking his head mightily on one of the bedroom beams.

I think we got our reward though when we showed them round. We'd not laboured in vain and their exclamations proved it. When we told them all we'd done in the time, I think they were really impressed and genuinely delighted with their blue guest room.

We only realised the next day that our first six weeks of 'retirement' had largely been spent indoors. Because we were so pale and had worked so hard, we intended to make up for it and enjoyed the next ten days as much as any we'd ever spent in Ribes. This was due, in no small measure, to the fact that Ruth and Joan are the perfect house guests. They fit in with any sort of routine, eat anything, go anywhere, do anything. They were also as fascinated by the Ardèche as we were.

We'd never been here in June before. The countryside was a revelation – the vines, covered in young leaves, the chestnuts just forming. On the way to the monastery at La Trappe the meadows on the high plateau were a carpet of flowers. Although the sun was hot, there was a freshness in the air which was simply exhilarating and very different from the sometimes enervating heat of summer.

There were only five other cars in the carpark at La Trappe on this visit. We were able to go into the wine cellars where the monks were working and buy some wine without queuing – an altogether different experience from our first visit with Hélène. It was the same when we went out to eat. Janet and Bernard had time to chat and show us round the wonderful new modern kitchen they'd installed as part of the alterations to the hotel.

We had Maurice and Georgette to dinner, lots of apéritifs with our neighbours and fun with the kids, Nicole and Ghiselaine. We walked, went sightseeing, lazed around talking, ate well both at home and out and generally spent a delightful time together. Ruth and Joan both said they'd love to come the following year, but this time in autumn for the vendange (grape harvest).

When they'd left us, we looked around to see what we'd missed in the general scramble to get everything ready. Roman offered to get on with tiling the backdrops in the kitchen and bathroom and Alan and I just pottered in the house and garden, adding little touches here and there, as the mood took us. And we finally found some time to read. By mid June it was starting to heat up and we reckoned the river would soon be warm enough.

Our next guests were all family. My mother, who'd never seen the house, was staying in Geneva with Sheila and her husband Raymond. They all three came down for a long weekend. I was eagerly awaiting my sister's reaction. She was the only one except the local people who'd seen the house as it actually was in 1963 and had advised us against it. She said she simply didn't recognise any of it except the old kitchen and *la clède* above, which of course we hadn't touched. It was true that there was very little resemblance between what we'd bought and what we now had. Told you so, I gloated inwardly!

At the beginning of July the temperature increased and with it the pace of our everyday life. Maurice and Georgette had grandchildren staying with them and we often took them down to the river with us. The girl, Dominique, joined Nicole each morning for the English lessons which I'd started earlier. Some of our French friends began to arrive. Jan and Bruce drove down for a two-week stay.

But our contentment was severely shattered when Ian arrived from Brazil alone, obviously very upset. We didn't quiz him but soon realised that it was unlikely we should ever meet our daughter-in-law, who'd refused to leave Brazil and come

119

with him. Ian apparently was due to start a post-graduate course in September at Manchester University. His friend Alan, with his wife and two children, was already there.

As it was also fairly obvious that Jan and Bruce were finding it difficult to harmonise their two very strong personalities, our very real happiness in that first summer of retirement was severely damaged. I've always said having kids is about 50% pleasure, 50% pain.

We tried to tell ourselves that our children were now mature, intelligent people who must make their own mistakes and live their own lives, but we couldn't help wondering where we'd gone wrong when both their marriages ended in divorce, and suffered helplessly for them both.

But that July we were still hoping that all would be well and continued to enjoy the sunshine, the river and the company of all our friends. For the first time I planned to have a party at La Clède.

When the day came I found it pretty stressful preparing a meal for fourteen people with the kitchen temperature in the high nineties. And in the evening the *mistral* decided to put in an appearance. After an interrupted *apéritif* on the terrace, we all had to squeeze round the dining table (for ten at most), rather than eat outside as I'd hoped.

Everyone had made a thorough inspection of all our hard work and it was generously praised. At 2.30am, after a massive wash-up session, we sat with our feet up drinking a last cup of coffee. We knew for sure we'd rather be where we were than in the most luxurious five-star hotel anywhere.

Our party celebrated for us the end of six years of effort. Our friends from Brittany were just starting their renovation at Bérias, and their party was to celebrate the completion of their new kitchen. It was essential that the weather be fine because we had to eat outside, the kitchen being the only completed room other than two rather primitive bedrooms.

Their courtyard was walled all round and had a beautiful old mulberry tree in the centre. It was one of the warmest, stillest evenings of August. Dozens of candles were set around on the walls and on the tables. The tree was festooned with fairy lights like a Christmas tree. I remember this as one of the most enchanting parties we went to. It was also the last of the year.

Our friends left one by one but winter still seemed a long way off as the sun continued to shine through September. We had the river to ourselves and had our last swim on the 15th on a baking hot day. Joyeuse was almost deserted now and the village seemed so quiet once the children went back to school.

On the 18th we had a heavy storm. The water in the river became much cooler. It began to be a little chilly in the evenings and darkness seemed suddenly to fall very quickly. Our thoughts began to turn homeward. I got out my files and started doing my sums, as usual.

We'd given 1,939F to Saboul, the electrician (he'd finally allowed us to pay him for several years' work). Again, the fact that the exchange rate was to our disadvantage was no fault of his. I'd paid the high price of 795F (about £70) for a kitchen cabinet I didn't like, 250F for the new bathroom flooring and 1,000F for our four dining chairs. I hoped these would be my last major purchases.

I began writing lists again – things to bring next year. Not as long as usual. A long garden hose for our extended garden, more books, more paint. We'd have room to bring more groceries next year – some of our stock things were still much more expensive here. And we wanted to come as early as possible, too. The garden was our next challenge.

We planned to get rid of our ancient fruit trees – new ones needed to be planted in November. Roman had promised to do that for us, but we had to clear the land first. We also had to make new veggie patches, as I wanted flowers only in the courtyard. We realised we'd really have to stay a whole year to get the land in good shape. But that wasn't about to happen so we weren't to be too ambitious.

We were beginning to look forward to getting back to

England and to seeing old friends again. It would be a new experience to find no work waiting, to be able to come and go as we pleased. An added incentive was that we'd decided to leave the noise and traffic of the south-east and settle in a part of England where the pace of life was a little less hysterical.

CHAPTER 11

BACK TO OUR ROOTS

We bought a newish house in a village near York. It had quite a large garden from which we could see the wolds in the distance. All around was the good, arable land of the fertile Vale of York, as flat as a billiard table. It would be difficult to find a countryside so different from the vineyards, chestnut groves and pinewoods of our hilly village in France.

We had a river here too, the Derwent, which flowed muddily along between low, flat banks, flooding the fields frequently to make shallow lakes. These attracted hundreds of water birds, which lent animation to an otherwise rather dull landscape, again quite unlike our steep and rocky *gorges de la Beaume* with its sparkling, rushing water.

The garden was as different as could be from our largely untended terraces in France. Our predecessors had obviously spent some time on it and we not only had easily worked soil, but trees, well-stocked beds and good lawns.

When we moved in on 1 March, the daffodil spears were already showing at the foot of the willows and silver birches. At the beginning of April it seemed as if the whole village had burst into bloom. Wallflowers, primulas, crocuses, tulips and narcissi appeared in every garden, but above all there were thousands of daffodils.

Those growing thickly on the banks beneath the old stone walls of York fully deserved the exclamations they drew from the tourists. In Farndale, an hour's drive to the north, five miles of riverbank were carpeted with wild daffs. It was a most beautiful walk along a narrow path with the green fields divided by grey stone walls and rising steeply to the high moors on either side. It was quite as lovely as the Ardèche, but it wasn't the Ardèche.

However, we were unable to leave for Ribes as planned, since my mother in Bradford needed some post-operative nursing. We thought of all the work waiting for us in the French garden, the clearing and planting we'd hoped to do, but found some consolation in our new English garden instead. It was looking delightful, ablaze with roses, when at last, in mid-June, we were able to leave it in a neighbour's care and drive south again.

Our dear French neighbours, the Hernandez, had planted strawberries (now over), beans, tomatoes and lettuce. Roman had carefully trained our creepers over the terrace and carport frames which were now in place. The mimosas were nearly up to the roof; the two oleanders which we'd planted the year before – one white, one red – were in flower and the second crop of roses was on its way. We had the beginnings of a garden despite our late arrival.

Any thought of major work outside had to be abandoned during the first week – we'd arrived in the middle of a heat-wave. For once, the house was uncomfortably hot; not until evening dared we open the shutters and windows, in the hope that a cool breeze would blow through. This was like August weather. During the day the most comfortable place to be was in the river and we spent most of our mornings there, usually alone.

A short, sharp storm put a stop to this and also made the hard ground workable. We commenced our clearing pro-gramme. Alan, sharpening his scythe in true peasant style, attacked the waist-high grass and weeds on the bank behind the house and cleared the creeper which was choking the quince tree. Armed with shears and secateurs, I began uncov-ering the steps and path at the side of the house. We then both worked upwards and discovered more steps and walls on the next two terraces – a clear path we'd never known existed right up to the road! It was very hard work – machetes would have helped – but so rewarding.

The worst enemies of the perspiring worker were the insects. Alan worked in gloves, an old pair of slacks and a sweatshirt, but I unwisely started off in shorts. Before very long I had at least half a dozen bad bites. Normally, we were not troubled too much by mosquitoes; but there are horseflies – a local nasty called a tâon. These and the odd hornet are definitely to be avoided. Two bites from horseflies had my leg swollen to twice its size from ankle to knee within half an hour. After that I was more cautious.

I suppose it was only to be expected that we should be attacked. We were hacking down growth, some of which had been undisturbed for 20 years or more. Although the heatwave was over it was still very warm. About an hour's strenuous effort was all I could manage. I then needed fifteen minutes' break with an iced drink and my feet up. Roman used to tease us about our easy life of retirement as we both flopped exhausted on the terrace in the evenings.

Sometimes it did strike us as a little crazy that we were struggling away with this difficult land in a grossly uncomfortable temperature while our neighbour in Yorkshire would be steering his motor mower gently up and down our lawn. Perhaps Roman was just a little impressed with our efforts on the quiet, because one day he offered to come and help Alan build up the retaining wall behind the house where Geo and Serge had left off.

It looked a terrible job to tackle – I couldn't blame them for not being keen. Where and how to start? The ditch was full of earth and the stones, old tiles and general builders' rubbish of many years. Now that Alan had cleared all the weed it was obvious that there were hundreds of stones in there, all of which would have to be cleared out and sorted. The best ones would then be used to rebuild the wall.

Fortunately, there was a certain amount of room under the new terrace. Moving along a yard at a time, a new space was made by throwing the small stones underneath , tossing the earth up onto the bank and rolling the good stones up against the house wall. Roman would then rebuild a section of wall – a lesson in dry stone walling given by a master.

Some of the stones were large and very heavy. Roman is not a big man, but only rarely did he need Alan to help him lift a massive stone into place. The most intriguing thing was that he would pause, inspect the hole he needed to fill, look around at the fifty or so stones at his feet, maybe knock a corner or some small protuberance off the selected one with his hammer, then grasp it, raise it first to his knees and then finally, with a sort of swinging heave, pop it into perfect place. It always fitted, without fail. It was then Alan's job to pack earth in round the stones and clear the next two or three feet of ditch before the next bit of rebuilding.

Throughout the four hours they worked, Roman refused to drink anything. He wore no gloves, but did admit at the end of the first day, when he'd been handling stones for almost eight hours, that his fingers were a little sore. Alan was exhausted but got into the rhythm of it the next day and was much less tired.

In two days they rebuilt nearly twelve yards of wall to a height of six feet. It was a wonderful achievement which we couldn't possibly have done on our own. We could now sit out the back and admire all our lovely old walls, which, according to Roman, were much older than the house. We'd also gained more light in the living room and kitchen and hoped we'd have no more problems with damp. Flowers could be planted on the bank to be visible through the back windows of the two downstairs rooms. We got more reward from this work than we could possibly have had from making and planting more permanent vegetable and flower beds, which is what we'd planned to do this year. Besides, we weren't altogether without those either.

We'd scattered a few packets of seeds round hopefully when we arrived – marigolds, nasturtiums and zinnias. The zinnias easily won; they seem to thrive in this soil and climate, so I've grown them every year since. Plus petunias and geraniums, inspired by Madame Hernandez' shining example. Her terrace always looked a picture, but with their help we were starting to give them something pretty to look at too.

As for vegetables, I've never tasted better tomatoes than those we ate from our plants that year. How they stayed upright with the weight of fruit on each truss was amazing. They were huge, bright red, juicy and full of flavour from all that sun. Just one would make a salad for four!

All the fruit and veg tasted wonderful and we wanted to grow our own, even though when each was in season, they were cheap in the shops and everyone else had their own anyway, so you couldn't give them away! You don't save any money, but it's such a pleasure to go to the garden and pick some beans and salad for the next meal.

We dreamed and fantasised about the garden just as we had the house, and we hadn't even finished that. We wanted to make better use of the cellars.

If we could get Geo to cement the floor – perhaps continue out to the carport – we could make a workshop and garden store. At least have somewhere else to put all the paraphernalia that had accumulated in the old kitchen. We'd used it to store just about everything from garden tools and terrace furniture to wine and trays of fruit. I'd cleaned it out thoroughly after giving the old mahogany bed to our friends from Brittany. We'd had a light installed too. Even in a heatwave it was comparatively cool with its thick walls and stone floor.

This year, for the first time, we'd ordered 100 litres of wine from the one remaining farmer in the village who made his own. All the others took their grapes to the Co-op. We paid £12 for our 100 litres, collecting it in a 10-litre *bidon* and bottling it up ourselves. It was only a light local wine – much praised by our Parisian friends as being "pure and healthy" – but not good enough to put down for posterity. We drank it a year old, or at most two, and 100 plus bottles, full or empty, took up some room and deserved a cellar!

We offered Geo all the old wood stored there – old beams

and doors from the refurbishment – as an incentive to get the job done. We'd done the same with the stone from the old silk-house and it had worked then.

Sure enough when I suggested it he was very pleased. Before we left that year, he came with his lorry and took it all away bar one lovely old beam we kept for the fireplace we'd restore one day.

We had fewer visitors this year. Ian was helping on a summer English course for foreigners at Manchester University. At Easter Jan and Bruce had decided to separate and she'd gone on a last-minute bargain holiday to Yugoslavia to "sort herself out."

When Ruth and Joan arrived in early September, the garden was not exactly a blaze of colour (theirs looked superb all year). The figs were ripening and there was the odd bunch of grapes on the old vines, but most of the flowers were finished. The excessive heat of July and August really seemed to burn them out, despite the endless hours watering. But we could show them more land now it was cleared and the rest of the countryside looked beautiful with its autumn colours glowing in still hot sunshine.

The vines were laden with grapes this year. Everyone said it would be a wonderful crop and a good wine – better than the previous year both in quantity and quality. The table grapes are the first to be cut, but before that was the chestnut harvest.

In the old days this had been the most important crop. Once there'd been no vines on the lower slopes of the village, we'd been told, only chestnuts, mulberries and olives. The vines had been higher up where now the pines had replaced them. Most of the olive trees had been killed in the severe winter of 1957 and not replaced. The mulberries were no longer needed for silkworms and the berries unwanted by the local people. There was still a chestnut market, but many of the farmers only picked a proportion of their crop to go to the Co-op, plus a few still for eating themselves, roasted or boiled. Most of them dropped in their thousands on the roadside.

At one time there was much more land belonging to La Clède, but it had been sold off as the previous owners got too old to work it. We had no chestnut trees ourselves and it was one of our cherished plans to plant some one day.

Through September it was warm and mellow. We went for long walks up in the woods, where the sun shimmered through the multi-coloured leaves. As we looked back over the village the vines looked brilliant, some of the leaves already changing to oranges and reds. Sometimes we walked the other way following the line of the river. Here, there were still some old olive groves which had survived. Not many of the trees fruited now but their gentle silver-grey leaves added one more colour to the kaleidoscope.

We asked when the grapes would be cut as we wanted to help. On 20 September, we went with Roman to cut the big black table grapes. It was such hard work. Roman watched me stop to rub my aching back and teased "Ah, it's too bad. As you get older, each year the ground gets further away!" I was just pleased I didn't have to carry on all day like all the other women working alongside the men. Anyway, we were pathetically slow in comparison.

The Co-op announced the date of the *vendange* for each village. The day they began it was bright and clear. Soon the tractors with their trailers piled high with fruit began to drive off one after the other on their way to Rosières to offload. All faces were beaming because of the wonderful crop.

We had a final clear-up in our own little patch of garden, marked out the sites for the new fruit trees, drenched the courtyard with weedkiller and began our round of farewell visits.

Our creeper over the carport was nearly touching the house wall and was a magnificent deep red. Alan had cut back the mimosa and pruned the roses the week before. The zinnias and dahlias were still blooming in all their various shades as we packed the car to leave.

"Next year will be our tenth anniversary here," I said to Alan, "but we're still not finished, are we?!"

"Easily enough for another ten years," he replied. "But we haven't done so badly to date."

I'd kept an account of what we'd spent on the house and we could now live quite comfortably in it as it was. But there was still the old wing waiting to be renovated and the garden needed hours of loving care. There was no question of resting on our laurels. The next ten years would doubtless be as frustrating and rewarding as those which had gone.

CHAPTER 12

TENTH ANNIVERSARY

When we first went to the rating office I was told that my rates would be 18F. "A month?" I asked. "A year, Madame," was the reply.

Even though we'd bought a ruin, it seemed impossible that any building could be rated so low. Later we found out why. The cost of education and the police in France is paid purely from central funds. Other amenities which we expect in return for our rates in England were non-existent in the village. There was no refuse collection or street lighting. But the most important factor we'd learned from the agent who showed us the house – we could build a double garage or a swimming pool, put in central heating, even a sauna, with no change in our assessment. Only a national adjustment of rates would affect us.

In 1975 we are paying 75F a year. We now have a weekly refuse collection and some street lighting around the church and café.

All the people who told us we were mad in 1963 now tell us how "lucky" we were to buy when we did and what a wonderful investment we've made. Most things, of course, look different with hindsight.

We can now see that the affluent years ended in 1974, though the previous ten years for us had seemed at the time to be filled with constant struggles to pay the bills. Through 1974 we feared increasing inflation and an ever falling pound, but we never for a moment imagined that inflation would exceed 25% and that the pound would be worth a mere 8F.

When we arrived for our tenth anniversary summer in '74, we'd already decided that further plans for improvements would have to be shelved. Even this decision was taken out of our hands because Geo was ill. No work had been done to our proposed cellar workshop and we were quite pleased to have no bills to pay.

Christian and Roberte had been married in February and were living and working in Marseille. Alain, the second Balazuc son, was away doing his military service. The old uncle had died, so the household was reduced by three.

Sadder still, the house across the way was quite empty. The Hernandez had taken a rented flat in Aubenas for two years so that Nicole could attend the high school without boarding. The other part of the house, round the other side, had been sold by the Torals to some people from St Etienne to be used as a holiday home, so that too was empty in May.

Saddest of all, the lovely house which Maurice had built because he'd been two weeks late to buy ours was empty too. He'd died suddenly in the winter and Georgette was staying at the Aix apartment.

It seemed very quiet in our corner of the village. Ghiselaine was a weekly boarder in Joyeuse and came to see us on Sundays only. The twins waved as they went by to school, but there were no games of *boules* in the evenings, no neighbourly chats on the terrace.

We remembered our village as we'd first seen it, gently sleeping in the hot sun; how we'd walked up the dirt track from the church. Now there were new roads, new houses and many more cars. Everyone had a TV and a washing machine. You could buy Mars bars and Jacobs cream crackers at the baker's and fish fingers at the village shop. Bruce, Jan's ex, had once cynically predicted that there'd be "candyfloss on sale by the river soon" – and he was usually right, that was the annoying thing! I prayed fervently against it.

In May 1974, as I walked up the hill on the way back from the bakery, I was a little sad as I thought of all these changes, especially the loss of friends. I looked at the fresh green leaves on the vines, felt the sun on my face as I looked up at that vivid blue sky. The pattern of the vineyards and the peach groves was unchanged, the mountains, slightly misty and blue in the distance, the cypresses still stood out starkly beside the church, the view was still breathtaking, the smell of the pines was still there to refresh you in the evening.

I looked up at La Clède and could scarcely see the terrace, hidden as it was by the now huge mimosas, but I could see Alan standing in the doorway looking out for me. In spite of the sad things, I was more than happy to be where I was, walking home with the new bread for breakfast at the beginning of our tenth summer in the Ardèche. And I blessed yet again those four people who'd prevented us from playing tennis one Thursday afternoon in August 1963.

SUMMARY OF MAIN COSTS

When	What	Francs
October 1963	House purchase	10,000
Easter 1965	Roof for old wing	3,441
Summer 1965	Sink, shower, basin, 3 windows and shutters	3,745
Easter 1966	Plastering, back windows and shutters, stairs	1,918
Summer 1966	Part demolition of lean-to and old silkhouse	883
Summer 1967	Complete demolition and new terrace	3,264
Easter 1968	New floor upstairs, 2 doors and shutters	2,754
Summer 1968	Septic tank and loo	998
Summer 1969	New windows and shutters upstairs, porch	1,823
Easter 1970	New ceiling in main bedroom, new wall downstairs	6,348
Summer 1971	Plastering upstairs; new floors in kitchen and shower room	2,280
Easter 1972	Bedrooms, bathroom, doors	8,427
Summer 1972	Back terrace	1,796
Easter 1973	Car port and terrace frames	999
	Total:	**48,676**

Extract from Surrey Mirror, April 1972

LILAC AND ROSES FOR SCHOOLS INSPECTOR

A LIFE of lilac and roses is waiting for Mr. Alan Anderson, following his retirement on Friday last week from his job as Senior Inspector of the Surrey County Council Education Department after more than 32 years.

Mr. Anderson has bought a farmhouse in the Rhone Valley at the little-known place called Largentière.

It is on the slopes of a mountain, and there is swimming and boating to be enjoyed on the nearby River Ardèche, a tributary of the Rhone.

The food is delicious, he said, and unlike many places in Southern France, there is no shortage of water in the summer months as there are natural springs in the mountains.

Mr. Anderson plans to spend six months of the year in England and six months in France. He will be abroad from the end of April to the end of September as there are many activities to enjoy in the French countryside in summer, but England offers more to do in the winter.

Mr. Anderson said that when he arrives in France in early May the lilac and roses are out together.

First county post

Mr. Anderson joined Surrey's education department in 1939 as assistant educational officer. He failed his medical to join the Royal Air Force and was then exempted service in the forces because of his specialist qualifications. He assisted in the training of the pre-service cadet units throughout the war. He became county inspector of physical education in 1943 and also did a lot of work with English and mathematics.

In 1967, Mr. Anderson became senior inspector. Although Surrey County Council is responsible for a smaller area than formerly, because of the reorganisation of London into the Greater London Council, it is still one of the largest education authorities in the country with about 685 schools. It also has over 100 centres for evening courses and more than five technical colleges. It also has Gipsy Hill Training College for teachers.

Mr. Anderson said the biggest change since he started work in Surrey was the improvement in buildings and sports facilities, the new visual and audial aids for teaching and the use of television, radio and teaching machines. Surrey has one of the biggest film libraries in the country.

Surrey's hopes

Mr. Anderson said the trend was to have fewer but larger schools because it enabled each school to offer a wider range of specialist teachers and equipment. The greatest difficulty was to find someone expert enough to run a school of this size. Surrey hoped to train heads and administrative heads in management techniques. Last summer the county ran a course at the Brighton College of Education for head teachers and others concerned with administration of secondary schools. About 60 people attended the course last year and it will be carrying on this year.

Mr. Anderson said he been working for a new structure for the inspectorate in Surrey which would now be coming into effect. There was now a newly-created post of chief inspector and then three area inspectors, each of whom was responsible for roughly one-third of the county. There were four staff inspectors, each responsible for certain fields of education, such as primary education, secondary education, further education and the in-service training of teachers.

There was a further team of 16 inspectors responsible for a particular subject and helping in the general work.

The Surrey inspectors worked closely with the government inspectors, known as Her Majesty's Inspectors. A representative of the H.M.I.s attended the monthly staff conferences and on the first Monday in July every year there was a joint meeting of H.M.I.s and all the Surrey inspectors. This ensured that the county was keeping up with national trends.

Mr. Anderson said that inspectors nowadays

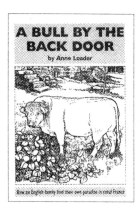

A BULL BY THE BACK DOOR

Written by ANNE LOADER
and illustrated by PATRICIA
KELSALL

An unexpected legacy enables the Loader family to buy an old stone farmhouse in the depths of the French countryside. It has been unoccupied for years but they are drawn to the charm and dignity lying under the grime and cobwebs.

Even before the purchase goes through 'Les Anglais' are welcomed with genuine affection by their new neighbours. From their very first day at St Paradis they begin to make close and lasting friendships in spite of the language barriers.

But it is not only their neighbours who welcome them. Soon they are aware that the spirit of the former owner seems delighted to see her family home being restored to life. Indeed, it appears uncannily almost as if she has chosen the Loaders for this task as she gives them daily "messages" about sentimental treasures hidden in the house.

ISBN 1 901253 06 6   Price: £8.99

THE DUCK WITH A DIRTY LAUGH

Written by ANNE LOADER
and illustrated by PATRICIA
KELSALL

This much-requested sequel to "A Bull by the Back Door" continues the Loader family's story. Renovations to their old house are going well but slowly, as they tackle every aspect of the work themselves. They have promised the spirit of the former owner that they will bring the place back to life but not change its character. She still seems to be with them as they get busy installing electricity, plumbing and drains – and doing the decorating. Old friendships prosper and new ones are made. Just when it seems everything is perfect, tragedy strikes at home in England and they face a period when just 'hanging on and surviving' is the simple goal. Their first test at St Paradis is coping with the coldest weather in Europe for a century: it's $-12°C$ outside and $1.6°C$ in the kitchen, the water is frozen, it's snowing hard and everyone in the hamlet is ill...

ISBN 1 901253 09 0   Price: £8.99

136

BUTTERFLIES ON MIMOSA

Written by
ELEANOR FRANCIS
and illustrated by
PATRICIA KELSALL

Owning a gîte in Charente-Maritime has been a far from humdrum experience for the author and her family – though they love their charming house dearly. Surprises were the order of the day and they learned to expect the unexpected. The purchase took place around Black Wednesday, their money seemed to vanish into thin air after being paid over, they had trouble with caretakers and eventually became astonished onlookers as a tale of arson and murder unfolded. Wayward sewage and occasional difficult guests were the least of their problems...

ISBN 1901253236   Price £8.99

OÙ EST LE 'PING'?

Written and illustrated by
GRACE McKEE

Busy pathologists Grace and Phillip McKee had enjoyed a love affair with France for years. Grace soon developed an all-consuming desire to 'do up' an old French farmhouse for their retirement in years to come. This led her to trick her unsuspecting husband into a property-viewing holiday in June 1992.

When she confessed, Phillip made her promise not to buy anything unless it cost almost nothing — and only after a long discussion.

A couple of days later they found their 250-year-old dream house in the rolling hills of Gascony and after a two-minute conversation, agreed to take out a second mortgage to buy it. It was in need of almost total renovation — a task that was to take the next seven years. Then events took an unexpected twist.

ISBN 1 901253 11 2   Price £7.99

All these books are available from Léonie Press, 13 Vale Road, Hartford, Northwich, Cheshire CW8 1PL (01606 75660). Please add £1.30 each for p+p.

La Clède, Ribes, Joyeuse, Ardèche

✻ Restored period stone farmhouse on hillside of protected
village – Ribes (30km to Ardèche Gorges)
✻ Spacious (100sq m) comfortable holiday home with beams and
traditional country furniture
✻ Sunshine, calm, beautiful mountain views, lovely river
swimming and sports activities nearby
✻ For walkers, cyclists, artists, nature lovers, sightseers,
food and wine fans
✻ Ideal for two couples
✻ Two double bedrooms + twin bed space, shower room/WC + bathroom/WC,
large lounge/diner + kitchen/diner (washing machine and dishwasher)
✻ Exclusive use of two furnished terraces (one covered), built-in barbecue
✻ Large terraced garden with secluded sitting areas in sun and shade
✻ Courtyard parking
✻ Prices include utilities
✻ Linen hire

**For more information contact Jan Bevan
Tel: 01227 458928 or
00 33 4 75 39 56 97**